GOD
AND GUNS

GOD
AND GUNS

The Bible against
American Gun Culture

Edited by
CHRISTOPHER B. HAYS
and C. L. CROUCH

WESTMINSTER
JOHN KNOX PRESS
LOUISVILLE • KENTUCKY

First edition
Published by Westminster John Knox Press
Louisville, Kentucky

21 22 23 24 25 26 27 28 29 30—10 9 8 7 6 5 4 3 2 1

Book design by Drew Stevens
Cover design by Barbara LeVan Fisher, www.levanfisherdesign.com

Library of Congress Cataloging-in-Publication Data
is on file at the Library of Congress, Washington, DC.

ISBN: 9780664266820

"We no longer read the Bible seriously. We read it no longer against ourselves but only for ourselves"
—Dietrich Bonhoeffer, *DBWE* 11:377

CONTENTS

    Approach to the Bible and Gun Culture   93
    Shelly Matthews

6. Can a Christian Own a Gun?   113
    David Lincicum

    Afterword   129

    Ways to Get Involved   135
    C. L. Crouch and Christopher B. Hays

    About the Writers   137

    Scripture Index   141

    Subject Index   144

FOREWORD
Stanley Hauerwas

I gave away the gun my father made for me. It was a beauti-
ful weapon. He carved the stock out of a hickory tree he
had cut down himself. At the time I was a student at Yale
Divinity School. I had come home to Texas for a brief
summer visit. The first thing my father did—my father the
bricklayer—was to put the gun he made in my hands. My
first words were "Thank you. But you realize someday we
are going to have to take these goddamn things away from
you people."

I focus on this exchange between my father and me
in a chapter of my book *A Community of Character*. In the
chapter, I suggest that even though my response might be
right given the place of gun ownership in American society,
my response to my father was despicable. I was clearly a
self-righteous little . . . (I leave it to the reader to supply
the appropriate descriptor). I had been away for two years.
I suspect my father sensed that I was becoming part of a
different world than the one I had been raised in. His gift
of the gun was a gesture of love. I was too stupid to get it.
I begin with this story of my father and the gun because I
think it embodies the tension with which the authors of this
book struggle.

There is, of course, as the chapters in this book
make clear, a tension between texts in the Bible that seem

to suggest that Christians are not always to refrain from violent means, though nonviolence seems to be the norm. Some may counter by pointing out there is nothing about guns in the Bible; but only a literalist would draw from that absence that the Bible might have nothing to say about guns. Any honest reading of the Bible must acknowledge there are texts, as these chapters suggest, that seem to justify the use of violence in a righteous cause. Yet there are also texts that seem to suggest that the people of God are never to use violent means to sustain even their lives. Both positions are there, and they cannot be reconciled.

However, the tension I have in mind—the tension also present in my father's giving me the gun—is the tension created by the centuries of the presumption that Christian have no problem with the use of weapons to achieve what is regarded as theirs. It had never occurred to my father that there might be a problem in owning a gun. And my father was a wonderfully kind and good man. That is the reality that the writers of these chapters face. They must challenge what has been and continues to be taken for granted by good people. Moreover, that which is taken for granted has shaped readings of Scripture that they must also challenge. No easy task.

The task is complicated because often the ownership of guns is not on anyone's agenda. For example, as one committed to Christian nonviolence, I am seldom asked about gun ownership. It is assumed that war is the main issue. But to own a gun is to rob ourselves of the necessities that force imaginative alternatives to violence. Of course, not having a gun may be dangerous but then so is having a gun.

I am happy to report that the chapters in this book offer the kind of imaginative readings that help us see what alternative readings of texts entail. In particular the authors challenge the familiar readings of texts that have been assumed to justify violence and the possession of weapons. They do so, moreover, by avoiding the gross characterization of the Old Testament / Hebrew Bible as violent in contrast to the nonviolence of the New Testament. As a result, these chapters not only commend nonviolence: they are themselves nonviolent.

That this book avoids that contrast between the two testaments makes this book important for questions about the ownership of guns by Christians. This book exemplifies the kind of work we will increasingly need to do and to understand if Christians are to learn how to live in a world in which they are no longer in control. That Christians assume they should have a gun in their possession is, as these writers show, a profound mistake given the witness of Scripture. This book alone will not change that behavior, but it is a start. Thank God for it.

ACKNOWLEDGMENTS

The chapters in this volume arose as part of a conference and public workshop held in Pasadena, California, in March 2019. The conference was made possible by funding from Fuller's School of Theology, under the deanship of Marianne Meye Thompson, and we are grateful to her and to the seminary for their support of the project.

We're grateful to Kyle Sears of La Cañada Congregational Church for participating in the workshop and for his leadership in the community. Melissa Hofstetter generously shared her time and insights during the planning stages.

A number of Fuller staffers, including Debbie Anderson, Linda Bass, Sarah Bucek, Kay Fox, Janna Gould, Bert Jacklitch, Sooho Lee, Bianca Puente, Faith Schierholt, Britt Vaughan, and Bill Wilkin, very kindly lent us their assistance with conference logistics and publicity. The Fuller Studio team, including Andrew Bucek, Lauralee Farrer, and Tamara Johnston, provided key technical support as well as handling the recording of the talks.

Dan Braden at Westminster John Knox helped us think about how to transform the talks into this published volume, and we are grateful for his vision and his personal support of the project. Natalie Smith handled the publicity with aplomb. Nicola Patton compiled the indexes.

GUNS IN AMERICA, BY THE NUMBERS[1]

C. L. Crouch and Christopher B. Hays

GENERAL STATISTICS

39,707   Total gun deaths in 2019, the most since at least 1968, the earliest year for which the CDC has online data. The CDC has yet to release figures for 2020, but preliminary estimates from other sources indicate an increase, to around 41,000.

36,383   Average number of gun deaths per year between 2013 and 2017.

100,120   Average number of gun-related injuries per year between 2013 and 2017.

---

1. Sources: Centers for Disease Control and Prevention (https://www.cdc.gov/nchs /fastats/injury.htm; https://www.cdc.gov/nchs/pressroom/sosmap/firearm_mortality /firearm.htm; https://www.cdc.gov/nchs/data/nvsr/nvsr68/nvsr68_06-508.pdf), National Institutes of Health (https://www.ncbi.nlm.nih.gov/pmc/articles/PMC4700838/), Pew Research Center (https://www.pewresearch.org/fact-tank/2019/08/16/what-the -data-says-about-gun-deaths-in-the-u-s/; https://www.pewresearch.org/fact-tank/2019 /10/22/facts-about-guns-in-united-states/), Everytown for Gun Safety (https://www .everytown.org/), Brady Campaign (https://www.bradyunited.org/), Giffords (https:// giffords.org/), Scientific American (https://www.scientificamerican.com/article/more-guns -do-not-stop-more-crimes-evidence-shows/), Time Magazine (https://time.com/5922082 /2020-gun-violence-homicides-record-year/); Council on Criminal Justice (https:// covid19.counciloncj.org/2020/11/30/impact-report-covid-19-and-crime-2/); and HealthData .org (http://www.healthdata.org/news-release/six-countries-americas-account-half-all -firearm-deaths).

Note this cautionary word on CDC *injury* figures: https://fivethirtyeight.com/features /the-cdc-is-publishing-unreliable-data-on-gun-injuries-people-are-using-it-anyway/.

12   Number of gun deaths per 100,000 people in 2017.

44%   Percentage of Americans who say they personally know someone who has been shot. The figure for Black adults is **57%**.

58%   Percentage of American adults who have experienced gun violence in their lifetime. This violence takes many forms, including being shot or shot at, witnessing a shooting or caring, and being threatened or intimidated with a gun, as well as knowing someone who has attempted or died by suicide with a gun.

RISKS OF OWNERSHIP

30%   Percentage of American adults who say they personally own a gun. An additional 11% say they live with someone who does.

67%   Percentage of gun owners who list protection as a major reason why they own a firearm.

Guns at home are **4** times more likely to be involved in an accidental shooting, **7** times more likely to be used in a criminal assault or homicide, and **11** times more likely to be used in a suicide than they are to be used for self-defense.

Firearm assaults were **6.8** times more common in the states with the most guns versus those with the least.

SUICIDE

61.2% Percentage of gun deaths that are suicides. The United States has a higher rate of suicide by firearms than any other country with reported data.

41% Increase in the number of gun suicides between 2006 and 2017.

5% Percentage of suicides attempts *not* involving a gun that are successful.

85% Percentage of suicide attempts involving a gun that are successful.

244% Increased risk of suicide in a home with guns.

820% Estimated increased risk of suicide in homes where guns are kept loaded.

74% Percentage of firearm suicide victims who are white men.

DOMESTIC VIOLENCE

4.5 M Women alive today who have been threatened with a gun by an intimate partner.

500% Increased risk of homicide in a domestic violence incident when a gun is present.

52 Women shot to death by an intimate partner in an average month.

13% Increase in domestic homicides involving firearms for every 10% increase in household gun ownership rates.

CHILDREN/TEENS

1,700   Children and teens killed by gun homicide every year.

8   Children or teens killed in unintentional shootings each day.

2   Rank of firearms among leading causes of death for children.

1   Rank of firearms among leading causes of death for Black children.

4.6 M   Children and teens who live in homes where loaded guns are kept unsecured.

3 M   Children who witness gun violence every year.

HOMICIDE

35%   Percentage of gun deaths that are homicides.

32%   Increase in the number of gun homicides between 2014 and 2017.

41%   Increased risk of homicide in a home with guns.

100%   Increase in risk of being the victim of homicide for people who have access to firearms at home.

8%   Increase in homicides associated with "Stand Your Ground" laws.

13-15%   Increase in violent crime rates over the subsequent decade in states that ease restrictions on concealed-carry permits.

RACE

Black Americans are **10** times more likely to die as a result of a gun homicide than white Americans.

A Black man is **15** times more likely to be shot and injured in an assault than a white man.

COVID-19

15.5%   Increase in firearm fatalities in April and May 2020.

30%   Increase in unintentional shooting deaths of children between March and May 2020.

42%   Increase in homicides across 20 major American cities in summer 2020, versus the previous year.

GUN CONTROL

85%   Percentage of gun owners who support background checks for all gun sales.

GUN VIOLENCE IN AMERICA: A THEOLOGICAL TREATMENT FOR A DEADLY EPIDEMIC

Christopher B. Hays

We are in the midst of a deadly epidemic. It has swept through countless public places, affecting all of us and killing thousands. In individual outbreaks related to gatherings for school or a concert, dozens have wound up dead.

We are speaking, of course, of gun violence, which killed almost 40,000 Americans in 2017, the most recent year for which there is complete data, and wounded about 100,000 more. These numbers are rising. Guns now cause more deaths in the United States than auto accidents.

The contrast between the public reaction to the coronavirus pandemic and the public reaction to the gun-violence epidemic has been as striking as it is perplexing. Americans have proven willing to make enormous sacrifices to help their governments and medical systems get control of an outbreak of disease—they have shut down the economy, canceled almost half a year of school, and given up all sorts of personal freedoms and enjoyments to which they are accustomed. Many take the threat so seriously that they will not leave their homes.

The sacrifices that would be necessary to curb gun violence would not be remotely as costly as those that have been introduced in an attempt to curb the coronavirus

pandemic. Arguably, these sacrifices would even increase
our sense of personal freedom, granting us greater domestic
safety and security. Yet measures to keep us safe from guns
get scarcely any political traction at the national level.

●————————————●

The notion that we could fix this problem is not hypothetical. Unlike the coronavirus pandemic, gun violence is a localized epidemic. Other developed nations have been relatively
untouched by gun violence in recent years. It may be true
that the United States, founded and forged in bloody wars
and settled at gunpoint, has a "special relationship" with the
gun.[1] As the figures in "By the Numbers" reflect, few Americans grow up outside the shadow of firearms. That was true
for me too. My own grandfather, a veteran of the Korean War
and sometime cattle rancher in Oklahoma, kept an assort-
ment of shotguns and rifles in a glass case in his living room.
And I found myself to have a relatively steady hand while
skeet shooting with the Boy Scouts. These are only a couple
of the countless stories Americans can tell.

From a different angle: The gun is a potent symbol,
and the United States has claimed gun violence as part
of its heritage in a way that other nations do not. Stanley
Hauerwas has argued cogently that "war has a role in the
American story that is quite unique. . . . [it] is the glue that
gives Americans a common story."[2] Is it unrelated that
guns are a domestic problem unique to America among
developed nations?

The United States' gun problem is also related to one
of its other distinctives: its enduring religiosity. Visiting from

1. *Lapham's Quarterly Magazine Special Issue: A History of Gun Violence* (January 2018).
2. Stanley Hauerwas, *War and the American Difference: Theological Reflections on Violence and National Identity* (Grand Rapids: Baker Academic, 2011), xvi.

France between the second and third Great Awakenings, Alexis de Tocqueville commented that "there is no country in the whole world in which the Christian religion retains a greater influence over the souls of men than in America."[3] Christianity in America may now be declining, but this basic observation was certainly true, compared to other developed nations, through the end of the twentieth century. Moreover, de Tocqueville also observed that "Americans combine the notions of Christianity and of liberty so intimately in their minds, that it is impossible to make them conceive the one without the other."[4] This is still true of the "Christian Right." And, although de Tocqueville had some positive things to say about Christianity, it is not clear that he meant this observation to be complimentary. After all, one of his first and broadest comments about Christianity was this: "The Christian nations of our age seem to me to present a most alarming spectacle; the impulse which is bearing them along is so strong that it cannot be stopped, but it is not yet so rapid that it cannot be guided: their fate is in their hands; yet a little while and it may be so no longer."[5]

If the spectacle of American Christianity in the 1830s was alarming, it is surely more so now. The inability of certain American Christians to distinguish American freedoms from Christianity has become dangerous—to the point of death. Hauerwas has diagnosed the problem nicely: "Americans continue to maintain a stubborn belief in God, but the God they believe in turns out to be the American god."[6] We are honored that Hauerwas wrote the

3. Alexis de Tocqueville, *Democracy in America*, 1.17. Full text available at www .gutenberg.org/files/815/815-h/815-h.htm.

4. de Tocqueville, *Democracy in America*, 1.17.

5. de Tocqueville, *Democracy in America*, "Introduction."

6. Hauerwas, *War and the American Difference*, 16.

foreword for this volume, and we hope that it contributes to his project of reminding us that God is bigger than our countries and ourselves.

The problem—which plagues U.S. debates on gun violence as well as on other matters of social well-being such as mask-wearing in a pandemic[7]—is that "American liberty" has for so long been defined in terms of "rugged individualism." Ultimately this devolves into "every man for himself," rather than a vision of the common good. Concurrent with the shrinking of actual Christianity, the United States has seen a rise in "Christian nationalism," a bastard stepchild that does not require people to think about their neighbors as human beings, or to consider the neighbors' health and flourishing, unless they conform to the "right" identity: white, Christian, straight, etc.

It is this Christian nationalism that ultimately underlies much of the U.S. gun problem. Crucially, however, Christian nationalism is less a *function* of participation in Christian communities than an *alternative* to it. Guns are part of that religion. Recent social-scientific research confirms this usurpation of God by guns among Christian nationalists. Mencken and Froese have observed that, "once embraced as a source of identity and power, the gun can become an object of worship which makes its own demands, no longer simply a tool used for emotional solace but rather a source of sacred meaning."[8] Physical actions like repeatedly loading, reloading, and cleaning a gun become ritualistic affirmations

7. "Christian nationalism" is in fact also a primary risk factor for unsafe behaviors related to the spread of COVID: Samuel L. Perry, Andrew L. Whitehead, and Joshua B. Grubbs, "Culture Wars and COVID-19 Conduct: Christian Nationalism, Religiosity, and Americans' Behavior During the Coronavirus Pandemic," *Journal for the Scientific Study of Religion* (July 26, 2020): https://doi.org/10.1111/jssr.12677. On the difference between Christian nationalism and Christianity, see below.

8. F. Carson Mencken and Paul Froese, "Gun Culture in Action," *Social Problems* 66 (2019): 7.

of membership in the cult of gun ownership, much like moving one's fingers along the beads of a rosary is a physical manifestation and affirmation of Catholic faith.[9] Such rituals reorganize participants' lives, both outwardly and inwardly, around a cult of the gun.[10]

It is thus no surprise that genuine "religious symbols and rituals may supplant the emotional and moral need for guns."[11] *Actual religious involvement has a negative effect on the correlation between conservative evangelical Protestantism and gun ownership*: those who attend church regularly and are engaged in their church communities are less likely to identify gun ownership as a significant element of their identity. President Obama's comment that a certain subset of rural Americans "cling to guns *or* religion" was accurate: God and guns are *mutually exclusive* organizing principles.[12]

My own activism has given me a small taste of guns' religious significance. A few years ago, I organized Fuller faculty to build and publicize some webpages with resources on gun violence. The project touched a nerve, drawing public attention. I had people calling my office to object; some administrators within Fuller started keeping uneasy tabs on the project, lest we claim that we represented an official seminary position. Later, when we planned the conference that gave rise to this book, the anxiety around security concerns was unlike anything in my professional experience. It was the closest I've come to the experience of cartoonists who make fun of the prophet Muhammad; it was clear that we were

9. Randall Collins, *Interaction Ritual Chains* (Princeton, NJ: Princeton University Press, 2004), 101.
10. Ann Swidler, "Culture in Action: Symbols and Strategies," *American Sociological Review* 51 (1986): 279.
11. Mencken and Froese, "Gun Culture," 7.
12. Mencken and Froese, "Gun Culture," 21.

treading on people's holy ground. I might have thought that my work on the Bible itself would have ruffled some feathers over the years, but nothing I have said or written elsewhere has produced this kind of reaction. Clearly, the Bible is nowhere near as sacred to some people as guns are.

•————————•

The grim sequence of shooting after shooting continues in U.S. news. There are the same outcries, the same calls for "thoughts and prayers." Arguably, the primary problem is that we simply have incredibly lax gun laws—it takes little time and little effort in most states to get one's hands on an arsenal of weaponry designed not for hunting or target practice but for war. Military-grade guns, along with firearms of every other stripe, are easier to find in some places than fresh vegetables. But the reason we have such incredibly lax gun laws is that even those who recognize the problem have proven politically incapable of doing anything about it. Even in the immediate wake of mass shootings, politicians take to Twitter to rile up their base, declaring that the "God-given right to bear arms" must not be infringed.[13]

Ultimately, then, the issue is cultural inertia—including (or especially) on the part of many religious groups. Many Christians wonder what their faith tradition has to say about this peculiarly American crisis. I have talked to numerous pastors who refuse to participate in community action aimed at changing gun laws, claiming that it's just too heated and divisive an issue. But a problem with such a significant religious component needs religious solutions as well as political ones. This volume is a start in that

13. E.g., https://www.politico.com/magazine/story/2019/09/04/yes-gun-ownership -is-a-god-given-right-228034.

direction, asking what the Bible has to say about gun violence in the hope of spurring our national conscience into action.

Thankfully, we're not alone in this project. James E. Atwood, author of *America and Its Guns: A Theological Exposé* and *Gundamentalism and Where It Is Taking America*, has been a pioneering voice in the conversation. Shane Claiborne and Michael Martin, in *Beating Guns: Hope for People Who Are Weary of Violence*, offer pastoral perspectives on the problem. There are also academic studies that investigate America's particular preoccupation with guns.[14]

But there is a need for *this* book. In the early days of its development, we checked out the competition, searching Amazon for variations on "guns and the Bible." Incredibly, we found nothing like this book. Then we tried googling "guns and the Bible"—and came up with a lot of poorly argued blog posts and other similar material. Even more shocking was that almost everything we found was from a progun perspective. Again and again, we found these authors at least nominally connecting their ideology of gun rights to religious beliefs grounded in the Bible. As biblical scholars, we knew it was time to speak.

In 2019, a group of scholars, students, religious leaders, and concerned church-goers gathered at Fuller Seminary in Pasadena, California, to talk about the distinctively American crisis of gun violence. What does the Bible have to say about the use of violence, and how might that connect to the use of guns specifically? What would it mean for Christian faith

14. E.g., Adam Winkler, *Gunfight: The Battle Over the Right to Bear Arms in America* (New York: Norton & Co., 2013); Thomas Gabor, *Confronting Gun Violence in America* (New York: Palgrave Macmillan, 2016); Lauren Langman and George Lundskow, *God, Guns, Gold and Glory: American Character and Its Discontents* (Leiden: Brill, 2016).

and activism if we took the Bible seriously on this issue? The scholars whose work is gathered here are people who have spent their entire professional lives studying the Bible, thinking about the sort of ethics and politics it ought to inspire. We discovered that we shared a common vision. It became very clear that we see the Bible's contribution to the conversation about guns very differently than the authors of those blog posts.

The following chapters represent the results of these conversations. Each pays attention to both the ancient and the modern contexts of the Bible, using the one to inform the other. They bring in breaking headlines, pop culture, psychology, and survey data, as well as cutting-edge research on the ancient cultures in which the biblical texts were first formed—first to understand the Bible, then to follow where it leads when it comes to the gun violence that surrounds us.

In "Scripture, Guns, and Psychology," Brent Strawn focuses on the book of Joshua, which is notorious for its depiction of the conquest of Canaan and accompanying strong "anti-Canaanite" sentiment. Though people sometimes justify violence by appealing to this and other biblical depictions of violence, Strawn suggests that the Bible is no more violent than our own blood-saturated society. Recognizing that we're projecting ourselves onto the Bible, he argues, is the first step toward limiting our own violent proclivities.

Yolanda Norton connects the public lamentation of Saul's wife Rizpah to the public protests of Black women in "A Mother's Lament." Like Rizpah, Black mothers have cause to lament the murder of their sons, who have been sacrificed as perceived threats to the social order in repeated acts of state-sanctioned violence. Like Rizpah,

Black mothers have been thrust to the forefront in the battle for accountability; like her, their actions are a reminder of the importance of public witness in establishing the moral value of marginalized lives.

In "'Do Not Be Afraid,'" Christopher B. Hays asks how the prophet Isaiah would respond to gun owners' desires for self-protection. He argues that, even in a context of existential national threat, Isaiah eschews violence—even when it seems to be the most practical option. This "impractical" response to danger is part of a prophetic message that emphasizes social justice, the futility of human power, and the importance of reliance on God. The chapter closes with a reflection on a French monk who prophesied his own murder but forgave his murderer in advance, as an example of nonviolent imitation of Christ.

In "Israelite Bows and American Guns," T. M. Lemos compares the symbolism of the bow in ancient Israel with the symbolism of the gun in contemporary America. Though separated by two and a half millennia, both the bow and the gun tie together violence, physical dominance, and hypermasculinity. Guns, like the bow, are the purview of dominant males and deployed against dehumanized enemies. This dehumanizing violence is powerfully critiqued from within the Bible, reaching its climax in the Gospels' image of a crucified, emasculated Jesus.

In "This Sword Is Double-Edged," Shelly Matthews examines three key passages from the New Testament that have been used to justify unregulated gun ownership. Rather than arguing that the true meaning of these passages is either pacifistic or militaristic, Matthews argues for the importance of an interpretive stance that recognizes within Scripture both oppressive and violent texts as well as liberating and pacifist texts. Rather than an anything-goes approach to interpretation, however, Matthews identifies the communal pursuit of justice and love as the crucial standard by which the saving potential of such texts should be evaluated.

Finally, David Lincicum plainly asks, "Can a Christian Own a Gun?" Though the New Testament does not directly mention guns, it contains a number of resources that help us think about the role that individual Christians should play in our broken, violent world. In that light, Lincicum argues that the gun is a temptation to arrogate life-destroying power to the wielder, which should be resisted by those who follow a crucified Messiah. Guns give us the power to kill instantaneously, and the New Testament does not countenance our seizure of such power—even in self-defense. We are called instead to be a *signum amoris*, a sign of love, in a world plagued by armed violence.

◆────────◆

Although the arguments made in this volume are bold, our expectations are relatively modest. After all, if presidents and movie stars have failed to make a difference, what hope do a few professors have?

In the end, we hope our witness will inspire others within the church simply to recognize and state clearly, to whomever will listen, that any Christianity that supports guns as a solution to social problems is not Christianity at all. As Hauerwas wrote, "The church does not so much have a plan or policy to make war less horrible or to end war. Rather, the church is the alternative to the sacrifice of war in a war-weary world. The church is the end of war."[15] We testify that the church is also an alternative to gun

---

15. Hauerwas, *War and the American Difference*, 68.

violence, and thus a way toward an end to gun violence. We are inspired by an example like Dorothy Day:

> [S]he practiced a form of prophecy: she spoke against the atom bomb on principle and refused to cooperate with the civil defense drills of the 1950s, drills designed to inure the public to the use of nuclear weapons. Despite its blinding moral truth, the case against atomic and nuclear weapons has never had any political bite, so the efforts were without political impact; they were a form of Christian witness for its own sake.[16]

As Americans we find ourselves in a historical moment when even small schoolchildren are being drilled in active-shooter response drills, teaching them that the terror of mass shootings in elementary schools is more normal than laws to prevent them. It seems blindingly clear that an alternative is necessary. We stand as witnesses to the alternative.

---

16. Zena Hitz, *Lost in Thought: The Hidden Pleasures of an Intellectual Life* (Princeton, NJ: Princeton University Press, 2020), 176.

Chapter 1

PROJECTING ON JOSHUA: YOU CAN'T WORSHIP BOTH GOD AND GLOCK*

Brent A. Strawn

"Psychologically speaking, the projection on others of the
onus for evil and unhappiness is remarkably universal."[1]

This chapter does not immediately take aim at guns or gun
culture. Instead, it begins with the issue of violence in the
Bible. In my judgment, it is necessary to clear the decks
with regard to biblical violence, especially the violence in
the Old Testament. This is true for at least two reasons.
First, people will sometimes justify their own violence with
reference to Scripture. People do this in different ways
and for different reasons; there is no one single way it is
done. Second, we need to address the violence in Scripture
because we might legitimately wonder how the Bible could
be used as an *anti*violence text if—as is certainly the case—
there is a good bit of violence in it!

This is true in both testaments, but I've chosen as
a focus text the book of Joshua, with its narrative of the
conquest of Canaan. One might suspect the violence in the
text of Joshua has always posed some sort of moral problem

* Thanks to Brad D. Strawn for assistance with the psychological bibliography and
to Paul Seay and Aubrey Buster for thoughtful engagements with an earlier draft. I also
thank the participants at the Fuller conference for their comments and critique, and,
especially, the editors for their assistance and patience.

1. André Lacocque, "A Psychological Approach to the Book of Jonah," in *Psychology
and the Bible: A New Way to Read the Scriptures*, ed. J. Harold Ellens and Wayne G. Rollins, 4 vols. (Westport, CT: Greenwood-Praeger, 2004), 2:83–92 (85).

for theologically minded people, but in fact the history of interpretation recommends caution on this point. To be sure, the conquest narratives have been utilized at many low points in Christian history and in terrible ways: during the Spanish conquest of the New World, for example, and in the Puritans' justification of the displacement of Native Americans.[2] But, as a contrary example, Joshua appears far less often in medieval sermons during the Crusades than one might have expected.[3] These varied uses of Joshua indicates that much, perhaps even most, of what is going on behind such use is a matter of hermeneutics, interpretation, and praxis. That is, the use of Joshua, violently or otherwise, may have more to do with what is going on *in front of the text*, in the reader—in her or his mind and, thereafter, in her or his hands—than it does with what is *within* or *behind* the text.[4]

Another way of putting this is that the problem of violence in the Old Testament, or more specifically in Joshua, has been somewhat abstracted from the actual details of the biblical text. Violence in Scripture is a hot-button topic, to be sure—frequently touted as offensive to "modern sensibilities," whatever those are supposed to be—but this conversation has often generated more heat than light.

I suspect that few people today would say in quite so many words that they love guns because of how violent the book of Joshua is. Nevertheless, I think that it is important

2. Christian Hofreiter, *Making Sense of Old Testament Genocide: Christian Interpretations of* Herem *Passages*, Oxford Theology and Religion Monographs (Oxford: Oxford University Press, 2018), 197–201, 211–13, see esp. 160–213, for what Hofreiter calls "violent readings"; also Werner Wolbert, "Holy War," in *The Oxford Encyclopedia of the Bible and Ethics,* ed. Robert L. Brawley et al., 2 vols. (Oxford: Oxford University Press, 2014), 1:376.

3. Douglas S. Earl, *Reading Joshua as Christian Scripture,* Journal for Theological Interpretation, Supplements (Winona Lake, IN: Eisenbrauns, 2010), 238n128; Hofreiter, *Making Sense,* 167–9, esp. 169, 181–82, 188, 184, 194.

4. For these three worlds of the text—behind, within, and in front of—see Sandra Marie Schneiders, *The Revelatory Text: Interpreting the New Testament as Sacred Scripture* (Collegeville, MN: Liturgical, 1999).

to ask whether Joshua is really as violent as contemporary gun culture is. If it isn't, then that removes a biblical plank from the progun platform. At the same time, this will also give us a chance to reassess the book of Joshua as an important example of violence in the Bible more generally.

This project might seem at first to be rather oblique to the immediate problem of guns and gun violence in the United States. But this look at the book of Joshua ends up pressing hard questions about our own violence and love of violence. In the end, it goes straight to the heart of the matter, because it turns out that our obsession with Joshua's presumed violence is, in part, a case of the psychological defense mechanism known as *projection*: it's a sign indicative of our own violent proclivities, rather than Joshua's.[5]

PROJECTION

In psychoanalysis, projection is "a defense mechanism in which intolerable feelings, impulses, or thoughts are falsely attributed to other people."[6] It is also called "externalization" because, through projection, "a person unconsciously attributes inner impulses to the external world."[7] So, for example, "a patient might deny feelings of

---

5. Note Wayne G. Rollins, *Soul and Psyche: The Bible in Psychological Perspective* (Minneapolis: Fortress, 1999), 43 and 53–54, on "the unconscious as a factor at work in text and reader."

6. Andrew M. Colman, *A Dictionary of Psychology,* 2nd ed. (Oxford: Oxford University Press, 2006), 606.

7. Colman, *Dictionary,* 268. Colman's own example is "as when a child converts unconscious angry or aggressive impulses into a fear of monsters or demons in the dark."

anger but be very sensitive to and preoccupied with angry feelings in others around her."[8]

In Freudian terms, defense mechanisms are the processes whereby "the ego protects itself against demands of the id."[9] As Nancy McWilliams notes, "[t]he term 'defense' is in many ways unfortunate," because "[w]hat we refer to as defenses in adults begin as global, inevitable, adaptive ways of experiencing the world."[10] That is, while there are reasons for why Freud called these things "defenses," an exclusively negative interpretation of the term or of these mechanisms is unwarranted. Not every use of a defense mechanism is pathological. In fact, post-Freudian psychology has noted that "[t]he phenomena that we refer to as defenses have many benign functions. They begin as healthy, creative adaptations, and they continue to work adaptively throughout life."[11] This is why some analysts speak of mature-versus-immature forms of defenses.

Nevertheless, defense mechanisms can and often do function in unhealthy ways. According to McWilliams, "The person using a defense is generally trying unconsciously to accomplish one or both of the following: (1) the avoidance or management of some powerful, threatening feeling, usually anxiety but sometimes overwhelming grief, shame, envy, and other disorganizing emotional experiences;

8. Stephen A. Mitchell and Margaret J. Black, *Freud and Beyond: A History of Psychoanalytic Thought* (New York: Basic Books, 1995), 27.

9. Colman, *Dictionary*, 194. Anna Freud, *The Ego and the Mechanisms of Defense* (rev. ed.; Writings of Anna Freud 2; New York: International Universities Press, 1966), 43, 122.

10. Nancy McWilliams, *Psychoanalytic Diagnosis: Understanding Personality Structure in the Clinical Process* 2nd ed. (New York: Guilford, 2011), 100. Anna Freud, *The Ego and the Mechanisms of Defence* (London: Karnac Books, 1993), 123: "use of the mechanism of projection is quite natural to the ego of little children throughout the earliest period of development."

11. See McWilliams, *Psychoanalytic Diagnosis*, 101.

and (2) the maintenance of self-esteem."[12] With regard to projection specifically, McWilliams explains that this is simply "the process whereby what is inside is misunderstood as coming from outside." She notes that in its mature or benign form, projection underlies the notion of empathy. In malignant iterations, projection can lead to "dangerous misunderstanding and untold interpersonal damage." She continues:

> When the projected attitudes seriously distort the object on whom they are projected, or when what is projected consists of disowned and highly negative parts of the self, all kinds of difficulties can ensue. Others resent being misperceived and may retaliate when treated, for example, as judgmental, envious, or persecutory (attitudes that are among the most common of those that tend to be ignored in the self and ascribed to others). A person who uses projection as his or her main way of understanding the world and coping with life, and who denies or disavows what is being projected, can be said to have a paranoid character.[13]

Two further points about projection should be noted before moving on. The first is that even if "a projection 'fits' [that] does not make it any less a projection"—although it is usually "easier to spot a projection when the attribution does *not* fit."[14] Second, it is generally true "that what people

---

12. McWilliams, *Psychoanalytic Diagnosis*, 101.
13. McWilliams, *Psychoanalytic Diagnosis*, 111.
14. McWilliams, *Psychoanalytic Diagnosis*, 111 (emphasis original). This is to say that finding violence in Joshua (or elsewhere) isn't *always* projection, even though the presence of violence in such places isn't necessarily proof that we *aren't* still projecting.

project is usually unpleasant stuff to which they then may
react with fear and distrust."[15]

PROJECTING (WITHIN/ONTO/AND) JOSHUA

The concept of projection has been used in biblical studies
many times. In what follows I want to comment on projection *within* Joshua and projection *onto* Joshua, as well as
the more general notion of projection *and* Joshua.

Let me begin with projection *within* Joshua—specifically, the notion of the wickedness of the Canaanites.
This notion is, of course, hardly limited to Joshua. It finds
some of its clearest expression in Deuteronomy, Joshua's
immediate canonical predecessor and plumb line for the
Deuteronomistic History. But the idea that the previous
inhabitants of the land of Canaan are irredeemably wicked
and therefore somehow deserving of their defeat is canoni-
cally even earlier than either Deuteronomy and Joshua.
It occurs already in Genesis 15:16, which indicates that
Abram's descendants will not inherit the land until the
fourth generation, "because the iniquity of the Amorites is
not complete until then." A little later, in Leviticus, we are
told that the Israelites must avoid certain practices lest the
land itself vomit them out, as it did with its prior inhabitants (Lev. 18:24–30; 20:22). The practices in question are
explicitly associated with "the nations" that God is driv-
ing out before Israel. "Because they did all these things, I
was disgusted with them," the Lord says (Lev. 20:23). In
Deuteronomy, we get the impression that the Canaanites
are highly dangerous, unnaturally large, and irredeemably

---

15. McWilliams, *Psychoanalytic Diagnosis*, 112.

wicked, tracing their lineage back to the terrifying giants of old mentioned in Genesis 6:1–4.

All this is a prelude—an important literary and theological preamble—for the conquest of the land of Canaan, which is described in Joshua and Judges. It is also ripe for analysis as projection.[16] As André Lacocque has noted, projecting the responsibility for one's own evil and unhappiness onto others is "remarkably universal."[17] It is also remarkably effective. What better way to justify brutal military action than to depict the enemy as demonic and therefore deserving of it?

Unsurprisingly, there has been significant ethical and ideological critique of the conquest narrative and its "anti-Canaanitism." Such criticism can come from academics but often appears in equally powerful forms among lay readers, whether religious, nonreligious, or even antireligious. As an example of the latter, Richard Dawkins has called "the God of the Old Testament" a "vindictive, bloodthirsty ethnic cleanser" who is "racist, infanticidal, genocidal, filicidal, pestilential" (and so on): in sum, a "capriciously malevolent bully."[18] In the religious camp, megachurch pastor Andy Stanley's recent book basically agrees with Dawkins and so blames everything that is wrong with Christianity on the Old Testament.[19] Among the academics, the author of a recent article on

16. Cf. D. Andrew Kille, "'The Bible Made Me Do It': Text, Interpretation and Violence," in *Psychological Insight into the Bible: Texts and Readings,* ed. Wayne G. Rollins and D. Andrew Kille (Grand Rapids: Eerdmans, 2007), 238: "When sacred texts develop to express and define group identity in a context of conflict, they often crystallize these idealizations and projections and preserve them in written form."

17. Lacocque, "A Psychological Approach," 85.

18. Richard Dawkins, *The God Delusion* (Boston: Houghton Mifflin, 2006), 51.

19. Andy Stanley, *Irresistible: Reclaiming the New That Jesus Unleashed for the World* (Grand Rapids: Zondervan, 2018). Katharine Dell also concedes too much to the New Atheism in her *Who Needs the Old Testament? Its Enduring Appeal and Why the New Atheists Don't Get It* (Eugene, OR: Cascade, 2017). For my own take on such things,

"Holy War" in *The Oxford Encyclopedia of the Bible and Ethics* blandly writes of "the fact that God is presented as one who delights in human sacrifice."[20] Sadly (or, rather, revealingly!), he offers no support—primary or secondary, theoretical or theological—for this stunning claim; neither does he make any mention of evidence to the contrary (e.g., Ezek. 18:32; 33:11).

In some of the preceding critiques we seem to have moved from projection *within* Joshua—on the wicked, evil Canaanites—to projection *onto* Joshua—or the biblical authors—by contemporary readers. This possibility has to be reckoned with, if for no other reason than the Bible contains differing voices on the matter of "anti-Canaanitism."[21] To return to Deuteronomy: yes, Deuteronomy 9:4–5 states that it is on account of the wickedness of the nations that the Lord is giving the land to Israel. "[B]ut this is little more than an aside within a larger rhetorical point where the clear emphasis is on the wickedness *of Israel*, not of the Canaanites."[22] Deuteronomy insists on the wickedness of the nations (9:4–5a), but it also stresses the importance of the ancestral promises (9:5b), before offering an extended sermonette on how stubborn and rebellious Israel truly is (9:6–10:11). This is further framed by two important remarks: first, that "you have been rebellious against the LORD from the day you came out of the land of Egypt until you came to this place!" (Deut. 9:7) and, second,

---

see Brent A. Strawn, *The Old Testament Is Dying: A Diagnosis and Recommended Treatment* (Grand Rapids: Baker Academic, 2017), 83–102.

20. Wolbert, "Holy War," 376.

21. Cf. Ernst Axel Knauf, "Joshua and Judges," in *Oxford Encyclopedia*, ed. Brawley et al., 1:451–54 (451): "The modern—and predominantly Christian or atheist—view of Joshua is based on a rather superficial reading."

22. Strawn, "Canaan and Canaanites," 1:109 (emphasis added).

that "You have been rebellious against the Lord as long as he has known you!" (9:24).[23]

Statements like these destabilize an overly neat-and-clean distinction between holy Israel and wicked Canaan. Importantly, this is happening within the pages of Scripture itself—even *within* Deuteronomy itself, the covenant document par excellence, replete with what many deem a simplistic form of retributive theology.[24]

When readers do not recognize this kind of differentiation and nuance *within* the Bible, they are guilty of a defense mechanism known as *splitting*, "in which a person segregates experiences into all-good and all-bad categories with no room for ambiguity and ambivalence."[25] Scripture itself, by problematizing its own distinction between the righteous (Israelite) and the wicked (Canaanite), is decidedly *not* guilty of such splitting.

There are numerous other exceptions to "anti-Canaanitism." Here, quickly, are five:

1. "Rahab, the prostitute, with her family and all who belonged to her," who "lived in Israel ever since" (Josh. 6:25; cf. Josh. 2), makes a notable appearance in the lineage of Jesus (Matt. 1:5) and is also mentioned in Hebrews 11:3 and James 2:25.
2. The Gibeonites trick the Israelites into making a covenant with them (Josh. 9) and live alongside them.

---

23. The Hebrew text has "from the day I (i.e., Moses) knew you," but "from the day he [i.e., the LORD] knew you" is preferable.

24. This is not to say that the "othering" of the Canaanites does not happen in Scripture (since it most certainly does), or that it is not problematic (which it most certainly is). See, among others, Jon D. Levenson, "Is There a Counterpart in the Hebrew Bible to New Testament Anti-Semitism?" *Journal of Ecumenical Studies* 22 (1985): 242-60.

25. McWilliams, *Psychoanalytic Diagnosis*, 103.

3. The Geshurites and the Maacathites are *not* driven out by Israel but, like Rahab and her family, "live within Israel to this day" (Josh. 13:13).

4. Several other similar cases: the Jebusites, for instance, "live with the people of Judah in Jerusalem to this day" (15:63); the Canaanites living in Gezer, who "have lived within Ephraim to this day" (16:10); and a series of towns that the Manassites did not take possession of, so that "the Canaanites continued to live in that land" (17:12). Such notices stand in some tension—to say the least—with texts that seem to suggest a complete and total victory of the land (e.g., 11:23; 21:43–45).

5. Finally, Matthew's Gospel recounts an encounter with Jesus and a "Canaanite woman" (Matt. 15:22–28; cf. Mark 7:26: "Syro-Phoenician"). She calls Jesus "Lord" no less than three times (Matt. 15:22, 25, 27) and, after meeting with silence and then two rebuffs (vv. 23, 24, 26), finally succeeds in beseeching Jesus on behalf of her and her child. Jesus ends their exchange by commending this *Canaanite* woman for her *great faith* (v. 28).

Taken together, these various accounts show that mercy can be shown even to those to whom "no mercy" was ever to be shown (Deut. 7:2) and also highlight that the archetypal "non-Israelite" Canaanites can—at least on occasion—serve as models of faith, even to Israel itself.

In sum, the Bible—even just the book of Joshua considered all by itself—is not nearly so uniform or thoroughgoing on the matter of violence, let alone ethnic cleansing or genocide, as some would make it out to be.

What is going on, then, when the Bible, or the book of Joshua, is made out to be that way by various readers?

Could it be a matter of projecting our own violent tendencies onto Joshua or onto the Bible writ large?

THE VIOLENCE IN US

If we entertain the idea that projection might be at work in certain interpretations of violence in the Bible, that would mean that we need to take a sober look not (only) at the violence in Scripture but at the violence *in us*. If *we* are projecting onto Joshua, then the issues are at least partially internal—*we* are the ones who are violent and warlike.

In point of fact, we are far more profoundly violent than anything found in the Old Testament. We are *entertained* by violence: we choose to watch it on television and in movies, to listen to it in song, even to enact it ourselves in video games—all for our entertainment. We choose to do this for our *leisure*, rather than something else.

Moreover, this violence—whether the "enjoyable," entertaining kind or the more serious, realistic kind—can hardly be said to be better than what one finds in the Old Testament. To the contrary, it seems far *worse* in at least three ways. First, our violence is increasingly *more graphic, more brutal, and more gruesome*. We see gun shots to the head at point blank range on broadcast television, for example—not just on cable or Netflix.

Second, our violence is *far more effective*. In the ancient world, killing someone was a difficult thing to do. The ancients had few long-distance weapons, and what they did have was not accompanied by an extended magazine, magnified scope, or laser sight. There were no hair triggers. You didn't kill someone, accidentally, with a

preloaded bow and arrow—there were no preloaded bows!
And in battle, if all else failed, you could always just try to
run away. Presuming that you were faster than your adver-
sary (or at least your next fastest comrade), odds were good
that you'd live to see another day. Not so in contemporary
warcraft—and I'm just talking about the warcraft available
at the local gun store, not even the kind undertaken by the
military. (Note, though, that the gap between the two types
is increasingly negligible.)

A third way our violence is worse than the Bible's
is that the prevalence of violence in our culture *makes us
increasingly desensitized to it*. How else could we tolerate
ever more violent entertainment—extra points for head shots
in video games, and so on? How else could we tolerate the
plague of mass shootings in our country? These disturbing
realities show that our own brand of violence is not just
more brutal, more effective, or more desensitizing—it's
also just *more*: there's more of it, all over the place, virtually
everywhere you look (and also where you don't).[26]

When we come to the Bible and say, "My, my, I'm
shocked at all the violence here," we might well imagine
the Bible looking back at us and saying: "Who are *you* to
be calling *me* 'violent'?" We must beware, that is, of a profoundly hypocritical duplicity—or, to return to our earlier
language, we must beware of being guilty of projection:
"*I'm* not violent, for heaven's sake, but *Joshua* sure is!"

Well, no, not really. Or at least that's not the entire story.

We, too, are violent, warlike. Any problem that exists
with violence exists, first and foremost, within us. This is
the first connection between the Bible and gun culture. Our

---

26. See, e.g., José Porfirio Miranda, *Communism in the Bible,* repr. ed., trans. Robert
R. Barr (Eugene, OR: Wipf & Stock, 1982), 73–74 on how poverty kills just as awfully
as shooting does.

violence outpaces that of Scripture; perhaps our obsession with violence in Scripture is a way to escape that fact, by externalizing it—relocating our own violent proclivities elsewhere as a way of defending our own psyches, and maybe even our faith, from the fact that *we* are the ones who are truly violent. Put more pointedly: maybe our offense at Joshua—or Deuteronomy, or whatever else—is just a way for us to ignore the remarkably effective, widely available death-machines we hold in our own hands, in real life and on screen.

VIOLENCE AND SOLUTIONS IN *BOTH* TESTAMENTS

A second point of connection between the Bible and gun culture is a bit broader. It is simply this: the two Testaments are united on the problem of violence. The New Testament, no less than the Old, has its fair share of difficult, violent texts. The book of Revelation is an obvious case, but so are various sayings or actions of Jesus (Matt. 10:34; 23:33–36; Luke 22:36; John 2:14–22 // Matt. 21:12–13 // Mark 11:15–17 // Luke 19:45–46).

The dismissal of violence as an Old Testament phenomenon, rather than a thoroughly biblical one, is therefore a matter of biblical illiteracy, willful negligence, or downright false teaching. It may also be a case of projection, given how many Christians want to identify with the New Testament and externalize violence somewhere else in Scripture—why not the Old Testament? That way the New Testament "self" is somehow not violent, but Joshua most definitely is.[27] "How crude, primitive, and *un*-Christian of that *Old* Testament," one might say.

27. Cf. Dell, *Who Needs the Old Testament*, 205: "We risk sanitizing both Testaments in an effort to make ourselves feel more comfortable than we really should."

But, again, this simply isn't true.

And this problem cuts both ways: not only are people who make such statements unaware of the problems that lurk in the New Testament (no less than the Old), but they are also ignorant of the resources that exist throughout Scripture—again in both Old and New Testaments—that might help us think critically about the violence contained therein (and in us). That is to say, there are canonical solutions, not just canonical problems, when it comes to the issue of violence. Projecting violence onto the Old Testament prohibits one from realizing and benefiting from these solutions. This is especially unfortunate, since the Old Testament's merits and solutions are both several and significant.

THE BIBLE WORRIES ABOUT VIOLENCE

As I noted earlier, projection can keep us from more healthy, integrated states. For present purposes, a healthy, integrated state might include a better integration of the two parts of Christian Scripture. It would also involve a coming to terms with our *own* problems with violence—neither externalizing them nor justifying them.

I am imagining a sober, rational reckoning with (our) violence and how to curtail it—stop it—somehow keep it from becoming pathological and pandemic. The Bible helps with this by highlighting how truly violent we are now, compared to then—and the Old Testament specifically helps by manifesting strategies of containment that limit violence in crucial ways. It thereby functions as a model for how we might do the same.

There is a reasonable amount of evidence that the violence of the Old Testament is not nearly as thoroughgoing or as "realistic" as some would have it. Consider Deuteronomy 7:1–5:

> Now once the LORD your God brings you into the land you are entering to take possession of, and he drives out numerous nations before you—the Hittites, the Girgashites, the Amorites, the Canaanites, the Perizzites, the Hivites, and the Jebusites: seven nations that are larger and stronger than you—once the LORD your God lays them before you, you must strike them down, placing them under the ban [*haḥărēm taḥărîm*, from the verbal root *ḥ-r-m*; NRSV translates this as "then you must utterly destroy them"]. Don't make any covenants with them, and don't be merciful to them. Don't intermarry with them. Don't give your daughter to one of their sons to marry, and don't take one of their daughters to marry your son, because they will turn your child away from following me so that they end up serving other gods. That will make the LORD's anger burn against you, and he will quickly annihilate you. Instead, this is what you must do with these nations: rip down their altars, smash their sacred stones, cut down their sacred poles, and burn their idols. (CEB)

If putting the Canaanites and all others "to the ban" means "utterly destroying them" (so NRSV), why would the very next verse forbid intermarriage? To quote R. W. L. Moberly: "to put it crudely, corpses do not raise the temptation of marriage."[28] If "the ban" designated complete and total annihilation, there would be no need

---

28. R. W. L. Moberly, "Toward an Interpretation of the Shema," in *Theological Exegesis: Essays in Honor of Brevard S. Childs,* ed. Christopher Seitz and Kathryn Greene-McCreight (Grand Rapids: Eerdmans, 1999), 124–44 (135).

for Deuteronomy to immediately forbid intermarriage, the making of treaties, and all the rest. The presence of these additional injunctions indicates that the ban wasn't practiced much, if at all, or—and here's a very important point—perhaps the ban *did not mean* total destruction, annihilation, ethnic cleansing, or genocide, after all.[29]

We might also consider this passage, just a few verses later:

> Don't dread these nations because the LORD your God, the great and awesome God, is with you and among you. (The LORD your God will drive out these nations before you bit by bit. You won't be able to finish them off quickly; otherwise, the wild animals would become too much for you to handle.) The LORD your God will lay these nations before you, throwing them into a huge panic until they are destroyed. (Deut. 7:21-23 CEB)

Paraphrased, the parenthetical aside in verse 22 says something like, "Well, come to think of it, this conquest thing is going to be a long process after all, because otherwise the aardvark population would get completely out of hand—and that would not be pretty!" If nothing else, this remark seems like the proverbial hedging of one's bets—a not-so-subtle hint that anti-Canaanite violence (or is it rhetoric?) just wasn't what it seems. Again, that hedge, this hint, is found already within Scripture itself.

Or, to return to the Canaanite woman in Matthew 15: Why is a Canaanite still around in the first century CE?

---

29. See Moberly, "Toward an Interpretation"; see further R. W. L. Moberly, *Old Testament Theology: Reading the Hebrew Bible as Christian Scripture* (Grand Rapids: Baker Academic, 2013), 41–74.

Maybe her ancestors were superfast on the battlefield, back in the day, and her clan's been running ever since! More likely is that this is more proof that the Bible itself knows of plenty of exemptions to "anti-Canaanitism." This one comes from the Lord himself, who commends this Canaanite's *faith* in him.[30]

If we don't know any of these examples, shame on us—but maybe the reasons for not knowing are more than just lack of biblical knowledge or awareness. Maybe we are guilty of projection. In that case, our lack of knowledge is more insidious—the issue isn't just lack of knowledge about Scripture: it's lack of knowledge about ourselves and our own violent proclivities.

Recognizing these biblical strategies of containment can help to prevent us from becoming desensitized to violence. If it is all violence, all the time, we get used to it: "Oh yes, another television show about homicide. Oh yes, another news report about another mass shooting. Oh yes, another mass shooting." If violence is contained and localized, marked as an issue and a problem, then we are *not* desensitized to it but *re-sensitized* to it—perhaps even put on notice regarding how it must be redressed.

To put this point most straightforwardly: the Bible itself appears to be worried about violence. Are we?

THE BIBLE AND GUN VIOLENCE . . . AND GUNS

This brings me to a final point of connection between the Bible and gun violence, which is to wonder for a moment

---

30. Strawn, "Canaan and Canaanites," 1:110: "Here, then, is another Canaanite exemplar of faith; and here, if nowhere else in Scripture, is definitive proof that the Lord himself sanctions exemptions to 'anti-Canaanitism.'"

about whether the Bible's violence, even that found in the book of Joshua, might help us overcome our own—including and especially the violence of guns and gun culture. This is a tricky matter. I want to begin by returning to the idea that the Bible puts certain constraints on violence, even and perhaps especially the violence in Joshua.

One constraint is that the conquest is not enjoined as a primary or even repeated metaphor elsewhere in Scripture—a point that could be contrasted, for example, with the motif of the exodus from Egypt, which appears frequently, across the entire Old Testament.[31] Indeed, references to the Canaanites are very rarely found after the book of Judges.[32] In the New Testament, the military metaphor is developed in Eph. 6:11–17, but it is entirely spiritualized: the helmet of salvation, the sword of the Spirit, which is the word of God, and so forth.

Another constraint is that combat and its prosecution are largely divine prerogatives. It is *God's* work, *not Israel's* work. That seriously limits any idea of replicating or reimplementing this violence, later, by human beings. In brief, it makes biblical warfare not something for human imitation but rather for *non*-imitation.

Considerations like these do not "fix" the violence that remains in the conquest narrative of the book of Joshua, but the biblical testimonies (plural!) on this period and these military endeavors are decidedly equivocal, and this prohibits any simplistic attempt to co-opt them as a means of justifying (gun) violence—unless we are happily (or unconsciously) guilty of splitting.

---

31. See Dennis T. Olson, *Deuteronomy and the Death of Moses: A Theological Reading,* Overtures to Biblical Theology (Minneapolis: Fortress, 1994).

32. Strawn, "Canaan and Canaanites," 1:105, which notes 2 Sam. 24:7 and 1 Kgs. 9:16 as the only exceptions.

All this suggests, on the one hand, that the violence in the Bible is not as bad as we may think. That doesn't mean that all violence in the Bible somehow gets a pass or is baptized or sanctified (though in my opinion there are legitimate means for the latter processes).[33] What it does mean is that violence is a truly complicated matter—one that the Bible itself is worried about and interested in addressing (if not fully redressing), through various strategies of containment.

On the other hand, it may be that the violence of Scripture is *worse* than we thought—not as that conclusion is typically expressed, via immature projection, or because the Bible's violence is worse than what we watch on television every night (it most certainly is not), or because its violence outstrips that of our own culture (which it most certainly does not). Instead, the violence of Scripture is worse than we thought—worse in the sense of more troubling—because it demonstrates how horrendously violent our own culture is, and highlights how few effective strategies of containment we have to limit our own violence. The contrast highlights just how brutal, effective, and extensive our own violence truly is—as long as we don't project all that onto Joshua or the Old Testament or the Israelites but instead reflect soberly on our own violent, warlike ways via the Bible's comparative light.

To be clear, I'm not trying to *minimize* the Bible's violence. I'm trying, instead, to *maximize* how violent we

---

33. E.g., through figural reading strategies, some of which may already be present in the text itself—see Moberly, "Towards an Interpretation"; Lawson G. Stone, "Ethical and Apologetic Tendencies in the Redaction of the Book of Joshua," *Catholic Biblical Quarterly* 53 (1991): 25–36. More generally, see John Webster, *Holy Scripture: A Dogmatic Sketch*, Current Issues in Theology (Cambridge: Cambridge University Press, 2003).

are, how violent our culture is, and how we ignore that when we project the problem of violence onto Scripture and locate it exclusively *there*.

There is one more important instance of projection that pertains directly to guns and gun culture. It is simply this: the vast majority (67%) of gun owners, by their own report, own a firearm for purposes of personal protection.[34] Protection *from what* or *from whom*, we might ask? The statistics are revealing: the largest category of gun owners is white males (48%)[35] who are not particularly religious, often less educated,[36] and who feel like they have lost economic or social privilege.[37] These are the people who, in places like Texas, flocked to buy guns after the election of Barack Obama in 2008. They fit a very specific profile, according to Jeremy Adam Smith:

> These are men who are anxious about their ability to protect their families, insecure about their place in the job market, and beset by racial fears. . . . In fact, stockpiling guns seems to be a symptom of a much deeper crisis in meaning and purpose in their lives. Taken together, these studies describe a population

34. Kim Parker, Juliana Menasce Horowitz, Ruth Igielnik, J. Baxter Oliphant, and Anna Brown, "America's Complex Relationship with Guns: An In-depth Look at the Attitudes and Experiences of U.S. Adults," June 2017, online at http://www .pewsocialtrends.org/2017/06/22/americas-complex-relationship-with-guns/.

35. Compare this with 24% of white women and nonwhite men, and 16% of non-white women (Parker et al., "America's Complex Relationship with Guns").

36. Parker et al., "America's Complex Relationship with Guns": "Like the gender gap, the education gap in gun ownership is particularly pronounced among whites. Overall, about three-in-ten adults with a high school diploma or less (31%) and 34% of those with some college education say they own a gun; a quarter of those with a bachelor's degree or more say the same. Among whites, about four-in-ten of those with a high school diploma or less (40%) or with some college (42%) are gun owners, compared with roughly a quarter of white college graduates (26%)."

37. In addition to the literature cited in the previous notes, see F. Carson Mencken and Paul Froese, "Gun Culture in Action," *Social Problems* 66 (2019): 3–27.

that is struggling to find a new story—one in which they are once again the heroes.[38]

In the words of Carson Mencken and Paul Froese, "white men in economic distress find comfort in guns as a means to reestablish a sense of individual power and moral certitude."[39] These are the kind of men, according to Angela Stroud, who own guns because they worry that minorities threaten their property and families.[40] Other studies have also demonstrated links between racism and gun culture. A 2016 study in the journal *Political Behavior* found that "[r]acial resentment is a statistically significant and substantively important predictor of white opposition to gun control."[41]

But this is an obvious case of psychological projection, because gun ownership among nonwhites is half what it is among white males (24% to 48%, respectively). Statistically speaking "[a] white man is three times more likely to shoot himself than a black man—while the chances that a white man will be killed by a black man are extremely slight. Most murders and shoot-outs don't happen between strangers."[42]

Consider another troubling statistic: gun owners with the highest moral and emotional attachment to their weapons are 78% white and 65% male. White men who have experienced economic setbacks or who worry about their economic futures are also those who are most attached

38. Jeremy Adam Smith, "Why Are White Men Stockpiling Guns?" *Scientific American*, March 14, 2018; online at: https://blogs.scientificamerican.com/observations/why-are-white-men-stockpiling-guns/.

39. Mencken and Froese, "Gun Culture in Action," 3.

40. Angela Stroud, "Good Guys with Guns: Hegemonic Masculinity and Concealed Handguns," *Gender and Society* 26 (2012): 216–38.

41. Alexandra Filindra and Noah J. Kaplan, "Racial Resentment and Whites' Gun Policy Preferences in Contemporary America," *Political Behavior* 38 (2016): 255–75 (255).

42. Smith, "Why Are White Men Stockpiling Guns?"

to their guns. This group also reports that they believe that owning a gun makes them better and more respected members of their communities. A remarkable claim, since guns are designed for one purpose and for one purpose only: not for betterment or respect, but for killing.

This situation doesn't seem to apply in quite the same way to women and nonwhite populations. These groups have also suffered setbacks, but women and people of color [aren't] turning to guns to make themselves feel better. "This suggests that these [groups] have other sources of meaning and coping when facing hard times" . . . often, religion. Indeed, Froese and Mencken found that religious faith seemed to put the brakes on white men's attachment to guns.[43]

This research identifies religion as a source of meaning-making and coping that stands as a positive alternative to owning a firearm. Religious faith, in other words, can disrupt attachment to guns. These are real signs of hope.

A similar dynamic of projection seems to be at work both in our own externalization of violence on the book of Joshua (the Old Testament, etc.) and in gun owners' projection of violence onto their perceived enemies. The latter are perceived as threats to gun owners' "stuff"[44] and must thus be met with deadly force—even though all evidence

43. Smith, "Why Are White Men Stockpiling Guns?" Smith's work, published in 2018, likely needs revision, especially in light of the increase in gun ownership among Black Americans, more so than any other demographic, in the first half of 2020. That said, according to a survey conducted by NSSF (the Firearm Industry Trade Association), sales to white women alone (16.6%) outnumbered sales to all African Americans combined (9.3% male; 5.4% female) with white men still accounting for a remarkable 55.8% of all gun sales during this period (https://www.nssf.org/articles/nssf-survey-reveals-broad-demographic-appeal-for-firearm-purchases-during-sales-surge-of-2020/, July 21, 2020).
44. What is this "stuff" anyway? In America, one assumes it includes things like life, liberty, and property—things that Jesus said were ephemeral and shouldn't be desired or grasped. See Matt. 5:39; 6:19–20, 25–31; Mark 8:35; Luke 12:22–34; 17:33; John 12:25; 15:13; etc.

indicates that, even if these people *were* real threats, they would themselves likely *lack* comparable means of deadly force. Therefore, most people who own and cling to guns for protection are, according to the statistics regarding most gun owners, guilty of projecting their own violence onto others.

What about the intriguing observation that much gun ownership and stockpiling is driven by the desire to be a hero? Here is one last point of connection to Joshua. Recall that there are mature and benign forms of projection; among other things, these benevolent forms underlie the capacity for empathy.[45] And so, as Kille notes with reference to the Bible, readers can project their own situations "onto the imagined world of the text . . . and thus begin working through to a healthier and more integrated way in the world."[46] Let us imagine for a moment, therefore, a benign, mature projection onto Joshua. In that text, one could see a hero narrative, of sorts—but one that is *already accomplished*, such that we need not pursue such heroism ourselves. Admittedly, the narrative in Joshua is at times violent, but its violence is severely constrained in terms of scope, duration, and re(ap)plication. In this light, Joshua might help us overcome our own violence—perhaps by (re) making our own violence less effective, less graphic, and less brutal;[47] by (re)making it *not* as something for leisurely entertainment, or something to which we have become desensitized, but rather as something far more serious: something that must be restricted, contained, *hyper*-localized—in literary form, bound in and to a book. Could

---

45. See McWilliams, *Psychoanalytic Diagnosis*, 111.
46. Kille in *Psychological Insight*, 238.
47. Earlier I noted the less effective weaponry of the ancient world; the modern parallel might be more effective, even extensive *legislation* to eliminate gun violence.

ancient Israelite "readers" of the book of Joshua have benignly projected onto it, to similar effect and with similar results, in order to *contain* their own predilections for violence? It would seem so: a lot of Canaanites continued to live in Israel, even "to this very day." One, at least, was still around when a much later Joshua (Yeshua/Jesus), this one from Nazareth, was teaching and preaching.

The narrative about this latter "Joshua," too, is a violent one. But this time it involves God's own son (Mark 1:11), who chose a disempowered way (Phil. 2:6–11), who did not call on angels in his moment of need (Matt. 26:53), who told Peter to stand down rather than stand his ground when the crowd came for him with force (John 18:11), and who did not resist the mob or his unjust accusers thereafter. This is the one whom Christians call the Prince of Peace, and every week, in the Eucharist, they celebrate *his death*—not his right to bear arms.

Given all that—the full sweep of Scripture, and so much more—how could any Christian worthy of the name love the idol of The Gun more than God? How could they care for the Second Amendment more than the Second Commandment? It was Christ himself, after all, who told us that we can't serve both God and mammon (Matt. 6:24 // Luke 16:13). A modern paraphrase might put it differently: you can't worship both God and Glock.

The prophet Isaiah's name means the same as Joshua's and Jesus': "The LORD will save." The LORD—not any other god, nor any gun. Isaiah's vision and enactment of that salvation, in our own time, remains out there, ahead of us:

> Then they will beat their swords into iron plows
> and their spears into pruning tools.

Nation will not take up sword against nation;
    they will no longer learn how to make war.
Come, house of Jacob,
    let's walk by the LORD's light.

Isa. 2:4–5 CEB

They won't harm or destroy anywhere on my holy
    mountain.
The earth will surely be filled with the knowledge of
    the LORD,
just as the water covers the sea.

Isa. 11:9 CEB

Chapter 2

A MOTHER'S LAMENT: MOURNING AS A WITNESS TO LIVES THAT MATTER

Yolanda Norton

In 1955, Mamie Till-Mobley helped set a new course for racial politics in the United States. Her fourteen-year-old son, Emmett Till, had been murdered in Mississippi by Jim Crow segregationists incited by accusations that Emmett had whistled at a white woman. In the aftermath of the tragedy, Till-Mobley ordered her son's body brought back to Chicago. She called on media outlets serving Black communities to cover the murder and at the funeral asked for an open casket, putting the disfigurement to which her son had been subjected in the course of his death on public view. "I want the world to know what they did to my Emmett," she declared.[1] As many as 50,000 people saw young Emmett's decomposed body in that casket on the South Side of Chicago. Millions more saw the photos, published in *Ebony* and *Jet* magazines. The sight of Emmett's body became a rallying cry across the world against the perniciousness of the Jim Crow South. Yet Till's killers, Roy Bryant and J. W. Milam, were acquitted by an all-white jury less than two weeks after Till's funeral.

1. *The Murder of Emmett Till*, directed by Stanley Nelson (Boston: WGBH for PBS American Experience, 2003).

Till-Mobley is but one well-known figure in the long line of Black mothers forced to surrender the bodies of their sons to the atrocities of the state. The litany of these women and their sons is long—too long to recount in this chapter. Among its more recent members are Gwen Carr, mother of Eric Garner—dead at the hands of New York City police officer Daniel Pantaleo; Sybrina Fulton, mother of Trayvon Martin—shot and killed by volunteer community watch member George Zimmerman; Maria Hamilton, mother of Dontre Hamilton—shot and killed by Milwaukee police officer Christopher Manney; Samaria Rice, mother of Tamir Rice—shot and killed by Cleveland police officer Timothy Loehmann; Lucy McBath, mother of Jordan Davis—shot and killed by Michael David Dunn at a gas station in Jacksonville, Florida; and Lezley McSpadden, mother of Michael Brown—shot and killed by Ferguson police officer Darren Wilson.

No charges were brought against Manney. Grand juries in New York and Missouri failed to indict either Pantaleo or Wilson. Zimmerman was acquitted. Dunn was found guilty of the attempted murder of Davis's three friends, but the jury failed to reach a verdict on the murder charge concerning Davis himself. Dunn's first trial resulted in a mistrial before he was eventually convicted of Davis's murder. The rhetoric around these cases—from Emmett Till to Jordan Davis—persistently foregrounds the purported culpability of Black boys and men in their own deaths. The widespread depictions of Black men and boys as criminals by the media have produced a national narrative of Black criminality into which even Black victims are forcibly inserted; even when they are murder victims, they are vilified.

Some of these Black sons died at the hands of the

police. Others, like Till and Davis, were killed by private citizens. Meanwhile the killers have been allowed to hide behind unjust laws that deem the deaths of these young men unworthy of judgment.

Perhaps the most shocking of these cases are those involving violent death at the hands of law enforcement. A recent study by the National Academy of Sciences (NAS) estimated that one in every 1,000 Black men can expect to die at the hands of the police—two and a half times the rate of their white male peers and among the leading causes of death among young men of color.[2] Although police use of force accounts for 0.05% of all male deaths in the United States, it is responsible for 1.6% of deaths involving Black men between ages 20 and 24. Between the ages of 25 and 29, a Black man's chance of being killed by police is nearly three times higher than that of a white man. Furthermore, there can be no pretense that this is a declining trend: the rate of these deaths at the hands of the police *increased* by as much as 50% between 2008 and 2019.

Although the NAS study was not limited to deaths caused by gun violence, the overwhelming majority of Black men murdered by the police are killed by guns. The lives of Oscar Grant, Michael Brown, Tamir Rice, Botham Jean, Stephon Clark, Rayshard Brooks, Philando Castile, Alton Sterling, Akai Gurley, Walter Scott, and a host of other young Black men are the human stories behind these statistics. The federal, state, and local governments of this country are liable for these deaths—not only because of legislators' persistent refusal to pass laws that adequately

2. These and the following statistics are from Frank Edwards, Hedwig Lee, and Michael Esposito, "The Risk of Being Killed by Police Use of Force in the United States by Age, Race-Ethnicity, and Sex" *Proceedings of the National Academy of Sciences* 116, no. 34 (August 20, 2019), https://www.pnas.org/content/pnas/116/34/16793.full.pdf.

protect our children from violence at the hands of others but also because government law enforcement agents play an active role in the perpetuation of violence and death against young Black men. Government law enforcement officers are sworn to protect us, not to kill us—and yet, killing us is exactly what they are doing.

Common to the stories of the deaths of many of these young men are the stories of their mothers: women like Mamie Till-Mobley, Gwen Carr, Sybrina Fulton, Maria Hamilton, Lezley McSpadden, and Samaria Rice. Each of these women's maternal grief manifested itself in activism for justice—a public demand that both the individuals and the institutions responsible for the violent killing of Black children be held accountable. For example, after Jordan Davis's death, Lucy McBath ran a successful campaign for Congress, focusing primarily on gun control. She now represents Georgia's sixth congressional district in the United States House of Representatives.

These women's activism stand in the line of the activism of Rizpah in 2 Samuel, one of the oft-overlooked women of the early Israelite monarchy. Rizpah's grief over her sons' gruesome deaths at the hands of the Davidic state prompted her to bold, relentless action—not only on behalf of her own two sons but also for the sake of Saul's other sons, who were also murdered by the state. Rizpah's actions ensured that these young men's deaths could not be ignored by the individuals or the institutions that caused them.

•———————•

Rizpah's story is not well known. She first appears as a secondary wife of Saul, in a brief episode concerned with the loyalties of the king's advisors (2 Sam. 3). Long after Saul's reign has given way to David's, she returns for a pivotal scene in the moral reckoning of David's kingdom (2 Sam. 21:1–14). The land has suffered under a three-year famine, and David seeks to end it in a bloody political bargain that costs the lives of Rizpah's two sons along with the lives of five other sons of Saul.

Making sense of the story requires knowledge of a broad swathe of the preceding material. Near its center is a tribal group called the Gibeonites, whose story is also not often told, though they are presented here as if they and the story of their encounters with Israel are already familiar. To an ancient Israelite audience, they may have been thought of as either immoral or as cunning tricksters, based on stories about them preserved elsewhere in the canon. Joshua 9, in particular, narrates how the Gibeonites tricked Joshua and the Israelites during the conquest of Canaan. Though the Gibeonites were actually indigenous "Canaanites," and so were supposed to be killed and driven out (Deut. 20:10–18), they pretended to have come from "a far country." They claimed to have been drawn by the account of the Lord's mighty acts in the exodus and so deceived the Israelites into contracting a nonaggression treaty that spared them from destruction at the time of the conquest (Josh. 9:15–21). Even after the Gibeonites' subterfuge was revealed, Joshua forbade the Israelites to violate it: the oath they had sworn was inviolable. But Joshua also cursed the Gibeonites, implying that God would avenge their subterfuge.

The story in which we are interested then begins with the revelation that Saul had ignored Joshua's prohibition (an ancient one by that time) and had "tried to wipe them out in his zeal for the people of Israel and Judah" (2 Sam 21:2). But now Saul is gone, David is king, and the land has been suffering from famine for three years. So David goes to inquire of the Lord about the reasons. He is told that the famine is a consequence of Saul's attack on the Gibeonites.

In an attempt to assuage Saul's guilt and bring an end to the famine, David asks the surviving Gibeonites what he can do for them—how he might atone for Saul's sin (2 Sam. 21:3). The Gibeonites demand the blood of Saul's sons, as representatives of his guilty house. Atonement usually requires an offering to God, who stands as the ultimately offended party (e.g., the Day of Atonement in Lev. 16). In this case, it is to atone for the breaking of a treaty sworn in God's name. Atonement is also normally associated with bloodshed—usually of animals but sometimes of humans (see, e.g., Num. 25:6–13).[3] David's aim is for the Gibeonites to "bless the heritage of the LORD" (i.e., the land).

So David responds by handing over seven of Saul's sons and grandsons, including two sons of Rizpah—Armoni and Mephibosheth. Granted absolute power over these descendants of Saul, the Gibeonites kill them, then bring the bodies to Gibeon to be exposed to the elements.

All of this is done with the full foreknowledge of David and his administration: the Gibeonites tell him forthrightly, "we will impale them before the LORD at Gibeon" (2 Sam. 21:6). Indeed, they go so far as to claim that it is not "for us to put anyone to death in Israel" (21:4). Responsibility for the men's deaths is laid directly at the feet of David himself.

Here Rizpah arises. Although she is unable to stop the execution, she uses her body to draw attention to the injustice that had been perpetrated against her kin: "Then

---

3. Daniel Lee McNaughton, "A Comparative Analysis of Three Versions of 2 Samuel 21:1–14" (PhD diss., The University of St. Michael's College, 2000).

Rizpah the daughter of Aiah took sackcloth, and spread it on a rock for herself, from the beginning of harvest until rain fell on them from the heavens; she did not allow the birds of the air to come on the bodies by day, or the wild animals by night" (21:10). The threat that birds and wild animals would devour one's corpse was a curse in Old Testament times, issued against those who are judged by God (Deut. 28:26; Jer. 7:33; 34:20). This vigil over the bodies—protecting them from the birds of prey and from the wild animals, from the beginning of the barley harvest until the rain finally came—is a refusal to let the dead sons be handed over to this curse. It is an outward sign of Rizpah's determination to gain justice for all of Saul's slain sons and grandsons, her own included. By placing her body where it served as a public witness, Rizpah also succeeds in drawing attention to the injustice that had been done; when David hears of Rizpah's fidelity to the bodies of her kinsmen, he goes himself to bring the bones of Saul, his sons, and his grandsons to be buried (2 Sam. 21:13–14). Contrary to the advice David originally received, it is not when the sons of Saul are killed by the Gibeonites that the land recovers—it is only when David buries them properly.

Has David done the right thing? On the surface, the story describes his efforts to appease the Gibeonites, who have been wronged as a result of Saul's failures. At this level, David appears to be taking steps to address lingering social tensions left over from Saul's reign; this, in turn, will alleviate the two communities' shared burden of famine in the land. Reading this text on this level follows an interpretation of David as a faithful and effective king—taking his early description as "a man after God's own heart" (1 Sam. 13:14) as a blanket approval of his character and later career.

However, this episode occurs near the end of the account of David's reign, and his later years are not portrayed so positively. Especially after the episode in 2 Samuel 11, in which he commits adultery with Bathsheba and then has her husband killed to hide it, his family and reign descend into real chaos. His son Amnon rapes his daughter Tamar (2 Sam. 13), and another son, Absalom, stages a coup and tries to take over David's kingdom (2 Sam. 15).

For good reason, then, many interpreters raise questions about David's conduct and view the story of his reign as one of moral decline.[4] Walter Brueggemann argues that the depiction of David in this episode with Rizpah and the Gibeonites functions as a climactic protest piece, strategically placed near the end of the story of David's reign in order to subvert any superficial impressions of Davidic *hesed* or faithfulness.[5] David makes an ostentatious show of sparing Mephibosheth, on the grounds of the oath he made to his father Jonathan—but in the very next breath reveals that he is willing to sacrifice seven other men (21:7–8).[6]

So David is not the hero of this story. Rather, it is Rizpah who calls attention to David's moral shortcomings. A woman on the outside of Davidic power, as a widowed secondary wife of the previous monarch, Rizpah is left vulnerable by Saul's and her son's deaths. Yet it is her profoundly personal loss and her resulting vulnerability that

---

4. Virginia Miller, *A King and a Fool? The Succession Narrative as Satire* (Leiden: Brill, 2019); Richard G. Smith, *The Fate of Justice and Righteousness during David's Reign* (London: T&T Clark, 2009).

5. Walter Brueggemann, *First and Second Samuel*, Interpretation series (Louisville, Westminster/John Knox, 1990), 336. The word *hesed* is often translated into English as "loving-kindness," but the Hebrew sense of the word is especially associated with expressions of loyalty.

6. The Mephibosheth mentioned in 21:8 is said to be Saul's son, who has the same name as one of Jonathan's sons (Diana V. Edelman, "Mephibosheth," *Anchor Bible Dictionary*, 4:697). This oddity cannot be adequately addressed here.

gives her the fortitude to challenge the king's supposed piety. In the face of untrammeled Davidic power, Rizpah's unwavering commitment ensures justice for the slain.

The narrative of David and the Gibeonites, in this reading, emphasizes the importance of publicly naming the moral shortcomings of our leaders—first and foremost, those who choose to sacrifice our children to violence. In the character of Rizpah, it witnesses especially to the public performance of personal grief as a form of prophetic witness, with the capacity to effect change by challenging the state in its failure to protect the vulnerable in its care.

•————————•

State violence in the United States disproportionately affects its most vulnerable communities, which are caught in a nexus of poverty, racism, and militarized policing. Alarmingly, the proliferation of gun violence specifically in these communities has been increasingly normalized. Whereas the sound of gunshots in an affluent white suburb draws immediate calls for help, a 2018 article in *The Atlantic* estimated that 80 to 90 percent of gunshots in poor communities go unreported.[7] This is due, in part, to the fact that such communities are much more likely to be inhabited by persons of color, for whom government law enforcement agents are just as lethal as the firearms on the street.

This pattern of selective attention is mirrored in other ways, with mainstream media outlets much more likely to give extended attention to homicide victims in predominantly white neighborhoods. When homicides in predominantly Black neighborhoods are reported, media

7. Krishnadev Calamur, "The Normalization of Gun Violence in Poor Communities," *The Atlantic*, June 24, 2018, https://www.theatlantic.com/health/archive/2018/06 /gun-violence/563582/.

outlets are much less likely to portray the victims as complex human beings.[8] "Whereas the loss of White lives is seen as tragic, the loss of Black and Hispanic lives is treated as normal, acceptable, and even inevitable."[9] In other words: when tragedy happens in affluent, predominately white spaces, we notice and then philosophize this violence as tragedy. When violence occurs in these spaces, we hold vigils for the victims and the nation mourns the senselessness of violence. We are summoned to such mourning in the wake of suburban, middle-class gun violence—in a way that we are not when violence occurs in low-income neighborhoods filled with people of color—even when people are unwilling to take concrete and sustainable action to resolve the issues that enable these horrific deaths: after Parkland, after Sandy Hook, after Pulse, after Columbine. We are unable to find meaning, because violence in these contexts is viewed as abhorrent and incoherent. In poor communities and in spaces populated by people of color, by contrast, violence is normalized; these spaces are portrayed as inherently unsafe and their residents inherently dangerous.

These disparate reactions to gun violence are a deadly symptom of societal racism, buttressed by ideological and theological convictions regarding the dispensability of the Black body. As Kelly Brown Douglas argues, the roots of the American state in a myth of Anglo-Saxon exceptionalism has "generated a theo-ideological framework to sustain the subordination of the black [body] . . . a theo-ideology that excluded black people not only from the category of

8. Beth Schwartzapfel, "When Does Murder Make the News? It Depends on the Victim's Race," *The Marshall Project*, October 28, 2020, https://www.themarshallproject.org/2020/10/28/when-does-murder-make-the-news-it-depends-on-the-victim-s-race.

9. Kailey White, Forrest Stuart, and Shannon L. Morrissey, "Whose Lives Matter? Race, Space, and the Devaluation of Homicide Victims in Minority Communities," *Sociology of Race and Ethnicity* 7 (2020): https://doi.org/10.1177/2332649220948184.

citizens but also from the category of humans."[10] Though the explicit identification of Black Americans as less than human may now be disavowed—in most parts of society, at least—the legacy of white exceptionalism continues to mediate the American response to gun violence. We exist in a space in which we are conditioned to rationalize the death of certain people—Black people, especially—as merely an unfortunate consequence of their lesser humanity. From the perspective of the state, some bodies—white bodies—are more valuable than others. Black blood is likened to bloodguilt and its expiation—its shedding deemed no more than what is expected and deserved.

———

Similar reasoning may explain the decision to begin 2 Samuel 21 with a report of the three-year famine. Natural occurrences were seen as God's response to human activity, and Israel's disasters were thus understood as the consequences of its transgressions. The introduction of the famine in 2 Samuel 21 establishes a problem: presumed Israelite sin, which requires expiation. This set-up effectively normalizes any action subsequently taken by David in order to redress the problem: a three-year famine establishes a context of scarcity that justifies doing almost anything to bring it to an end.

David is then told that the famine is the result of Saul's murderous betrayal of the treaty with the Gibeonites—that it is, in fact, a consequence of sin. But Saul's actions were not any ordinary kind of sin—there is no greater sin than the destruction of human life. The consequences of such

10. Kelly Brown Douglas, *Stand Your Ground: Black Bodies and the Justice of God* (Maryknoll, NY: Orbis, 2015), 51.

destruction are articulated in terms of bloodguilt: that is, the accountability for the (unnecessary) taking of a human life. The seriousness of killing, as well as its consequences, are established already in Genesis 9:6—long before the narrative recounts any more formal legal strictures. Still reeling from the flood, Noah is warned that to shed human blood is not any ordinary crime, but a crime against God: for "in his own image God made humankind." The guilt incurred as a result of such heinous action can be expiated only by the blood of the murderer himself: "Whoever sheds the blood of a human, by a human shall that person's blood be shed." The severity of the crime is underlined again in the legal materials of Exodus and Deuteronomy. In these laws, the purposeful shedding of human blood requires the community to execute the murderer: "Whoever strikes a person mortally shall be put to death. If it was not premeditated, but came about by an act of God, then I will appoint for you a place to which the killer may flee. But if someone willfully attacks and kills another by treachery, you shall take the killer from my altar for execution" (Exod. 21:12–14; compare Deut. 19:11–13). Any loss of life— the shedding of human blood—requires that some kind of consequence be imposed upon the perpetrator. The *intentional* taking of life mandates the most extreme form of retributive justice: the blood of the aggressor.[11]

The significance of human bloodshed arises from two seemingly contradictory capacities of blood: it can contaminate, but it can also cleanse.[12] Its effects depend

11. Bloodguilt may also be incurred for negligent behavior that leads to death—failure to guard a goring ox, such that the ox kills a person (Exod. 21:9), failure to warn an individual about a threat to their lives (Ezek. 33:6), or failure to fulfill an oath to protect someone from death (Josh. 21:9).

12. William K. Gilders, *Blood Ritual in the Hebrew Bible: Meaning and Power* (Baltimore: Johns Hopkins University Press, 2004), 95.

on the circumstances: the blood of an innocent defiles the earth, but the blood of the guilty purges the offense and relieves its consequences. According to Numbers 35:33–34, the potential scope of blood contamination is large—it can defile and affect an entire community. In 2 Samuel 21, this is what is thought to be causing the famine: the land itself abhors moral impropriety and has revolted against it in the form of a famine. God will not dwell in polluted places or communities, and without divine sustenance the land is unable to produce. Saul's offense against the Gibeonites explains where the bloodguilt causing this famine came from. In the process, it also rationalizes the subsequent sacrifice of members of Saul's lineage: the shedding of the blood of Saul's descendants is conceived of as a necessary result of Saul's own bloodguilt—as the only action that can undo it.

With David's permission, seven victims are "impaled on the mountain before the LORD" (2 Sam. 21:9). The author's note that these men were killed "in the presence of the LORD" acknowledges the ritualized religious context of the killings. The fate of Rizpah and her sons is determined by David's encounter with God; there is no one to confirm or deny the revelation to David that responsibility for the famine lies at Saul's doorstep, no one with the authority to save her sons from the system David rules.

After the death of her sons, Rizpah has nothing to gain, but nothing to lose: she is a mother of children that live no more, stripped of every man who might have provided her with the financial and social security necessary for survival in the unstable, patriarchal world of David's kingdom.

Although we are told little of Rizpah's motivations, and she appears on the surface to be uninterested in the political factors involved in the death of her and Merab's sons, her public lamentation draws attention to David's actions and implicitly calls them into question. Unable to remove the bodies from the stakes upon which they are impaled, she installs herself as a permanent fixture beside them, sitting on sackcloth—the material of mourning—and protecting them by her presence from birds of prey and other scavengers. Her public display of mourning draws attention to David's complicity in their lack of a proper burial; to be deprived of a proper burial and its assurance of the community of one's family was one of the most dreaded fates in ancient Israel.

Rizpah's actions thus call David's "funerary ethics" into question. Most immediately, by spotlighting his (in)action vis-à-vis her and Merab's sons, but also—as the narrative soon reveals—by drawing renewed attention to the deaths of Saul and Jonathan and the mistreatment of their bodies earlier in the narrative (1 Sam. 31). Mourning thus has the capacity to effect social and moral change.[13] In Rizpah's case, it indeed proved highly effective. When David learns of Rizpah's vigil, it impels him to act on behalf of his kingdom's proliferating dead; he orders not only that the men's bodies be retrieved for burial, but that they be placed in an ancestral tomb—an ideal location for burial, where the dead could be "gathered to their ancestors."[14] David's actions are not limited only to the young men who had most recently died: Rizpah's lamentation over her own sons

13. Gary Ebersole, "The Function of Ritual Weeping Revisited: Affective Expression and Moral Discourse," *History of Religions* 39 (2000): 245.

14. Saul M. Olyan, "Some Neglected Aspects of Israelite Interment Ideology," *Journal of Biblical Literature* 124 (2005): 601–16; Christopher B. Hays, "Death and Burial in the Iron Age Levant," in *Behind the Scenes of the Old Testament: Cultural, Social, and Historical Contexts of Ancient Israel*, ed. Jonathan S. Greer, John W. Hilber, and John H. Walton (Grand Rapids: Baker Academic, 2018).

has much wider repercussions, as it pressures David into retrieving the bones of Jonathan and Saul as well. Rizpah's very name ("glowing coal") signals her significance in the narrative of David's reign—she signifies burning judgment on the king, for his willingness to sacrifice innocent men for his own purposes.[15] As noted above, it is only when David buries Saul and his sons properly that the famine lifts and the land recovers—*not* when he hands the sons over to be killed.

⎯⎯⎯⎯•⎯⎯⎯⎯

American gun culture has, again and again, demonstrated its own willingness to sacrifice Black bodies to its own purposes. Again and again, Black victims of gun crime are depicted as though they somehow deserved their fate: Trayvon Martin wore a hoodie, so he must have been a drug-dealing thug; Jordan Davis and his friends were playing loud hip-hop music, so they must have been a threat. In these accounts, there is no need to acknowledge that we have labeled Black bodies *as such* a threat. If twelve-year-old Tamir Rice was playing with a toy that looked like a gun, we don't have to admit that the overwhelming depiction of Black men and boys as criminals by the mainstream media means that "in a game of cops and robbers, little black boys will always be the latter."[16] Racist laws, racist institutions, and a sociopolitical climate that prioritizes white rights over Black lives provide cover for the violent disposal of people who are inconvenient to the story that white America wants

15. Ekaterina Kozlova has suggested that "the glowing coals/dying embers idiom signals the author's disapproval of the disposed house" (*Maternal Grief in the Hebrew Bible* [Oxford: Oxford University Press, 2017], 12).

16. Javon Johnson, "cuz he's black," filmed at the 2013 National Poetry Slam in Boston, https://www.youtube.com/watch?v=u9Wf8y_5Yn4.

to tell—a story about equal opportunity, about freedom, about liberty and justice for all. The American legal system is predicated on a myth: that those who are in power have the best interests of *all* Americans at heart. To claim that the function of government is to protect the greatest number of people in the greatest number of ways leaves the door wide open for those who believe in this myth to sacrifice those who have already been disempowered as the scapegoats of our broken social order.

The ways in which we speak about gun violence in this country expose the fact that we have already decided, in our collective moral consciousness, that certain people and certain places are inherently dangerous and immoral—and that this immorality deserves to be purged through the shedding of blood. The national conversation about gun culture as a moral evil, such as it is, is predicated on a myth of safety. This myth holds true only for those who are privileged enough to see it rarely challenged—those who live in predominantly white, predominantly affluent neighborhoods, where a call to the police is a lifeline rather than a death sentence. Mass shootings in such neighborhoods are truly horrifying—but so is every shooting. It is only our willingness to distance ourselves from communities that do not have the privilege of living in such neighborhoods that allows (some of) us to maintain the illusion of safety that these violent acts disrupt. Those who live in neighborhoods deemed dangerous and immoral have long been deprived of any illusion of safety.

Rizpah's public display of grief calls the king to task for his violence. So, too, when Lezley McSpadden stood on the streets of Ferguson, Missouri, in protest at the murder of her son Michael, we recognized her tears as judgment on the moral failure of our nation. The lamentation of

Allison Jean, whose son Botham was murdered by an off-duty police officer in Dallas, stands in the way of pretending that American gun violence is only a matter of guns on the street. Like Rizpah's protest, these maternal witnesses remind us that the human proclivity toward violence is deeply embedded in the state, in the moral failures of leaders and power brokers, and in the willingness of a people to sacrifice the bodies of the marginalized to maintain a myth of equal justice for all.

Rizpah's story reminds us that mourning can be prophetic. In a society where the right to own a gun is more important than the human right to live, we cannot ignore her summons—and our responsibility—to mourn the dead, witnessing to their lives and against the system that cut them short. By persistence in public lamentation, our vigils and our tears will move our leaders to honor those who have died, and then act to prevent the deaths of others. Rizpah's tears force us to attend to our sins and summon us to repent. They encourage us to act and give us hope that, one day, America's own Davids will be shamed into fixing the real problems, into regulating guns—not only those in the hands of civilians but also those wielded by soldiers, police officers, and other agents of the state. Only then will the bodies and bones of those who have died be laid truly to rest.

Chapter 3

"DO NOT BE AFRAID": THE WALLS OF JERUSALEM AND THE GUNS OF AMERICA

Christopher B. Hays

People in the United States say they want guns to protect themselves.[1] Self-defense is the primary reason given for gun ownership, by an overwhelming margin, and women frequently cite protection as their *only* reason for owning a gun. Gun sales rise after mass shootings.

If information could fix this country's gun problem, one could simply point to the fact that owning a gun does not make people safer: Those who have access to firearms at home are (statistically speaking) nearly twice as likely to be murdered as people who do not, and firearm assaults are 6.8 times more common in the states with the most guns versus those with the least.[2] States with more permissive gun laws see more mass shootings.[3] More guns equal more death.[4]

1. Kim Parker, Juliana Menasce Horowitz, Ruth Igielnik, J. Baxter Oliphant, and Anna Brown, "America's Complex Relationship with Guns: An In-depth Look at the Attitudes and Experiences of U.S. Adults," Pew Research Center, June 22 2017, http://www.pewsocialtrends.org/2017/06/22/americas-complex-relationship-with-guns/.

2. Melinda Wenner Moyer, "More Guns Do Not Stop More Crimes, Evidence Shows," *Scientific American* (October 1, 2017): 54–63; see also Arthur L. Kellermann and Donald T. Reay, "Protection or Peril?," *The New England Journal of Medicine* 314 (1986):1157–60.

3. Paul M. Reeping, Magdalena Cerdá, Bindu Kalesan, Douglas J. Wiebe, Sandro Galea, Charles C. Branas, "State Gun Laws, Gun Ownership, and Mass Shootings in the US: Cross Sectional Time Series," *British Medical Journal* (2019) 364: l542.

4. "Homicide," Harvard Injury Control Research Center, www.hsph.harvard.edu/hicrc/firearms-research/guns-and-death/.

It makes sense to begin with such data, but we can't end there. Data does not speak very loudly to those for whom guns are a symbol of powerful justice. We have to change hearts, renew minds, and open eyes. Theology has a role to play in that process. Christian theology is particularly relevant: in the United States, those who call themselves Christians are more likely to own guns than those who do not.[5] Conservative Christian pundits speak of "a biblical right of self-defense."[6] It's not surprising, then, that a recent study concluded that "rational public safety calculations" alone will not be effective in changing American attitudes about guns: "attempts to reform existing gun laws must attend to the deeper cultural and religious identities that undergird Americans' beliefs about gun control."[7]

It may comfort dismayed Christians that this association between guns and Christian faith appears to be superficial. A fascinating recent study looked more deeply at American's attachment to guns and concluded that actual *involvement* in religion is *negatively* correlated with a person's psychological and ideological reliance on guns.[8]

---

5. Robert Yamane, "Awash in a Sea of Faith and Firearms: Rediscovering the Con-nection between Religion and Gun Ownership in America," *Journal for the Scientific Study of Religion* 55 (2016): 622–36; Stephen M. Merino, "God and Guns: Examining Religious Influences on Gun Control Attitudes in the United States," *Religions* 9 (2018): 189, https://doi.org/10.3390/rel9060189.

6. See Paul Stanley, "David Barton on Gun Control: Citizens Have 'Biblical Right to Self-Defense,'" *The Christian Post*, December 20, 2012, www.christianpost.com/news /david-barton-on-gun-control-citizens-have-biblical-right-to-self-defense-86978/; Mary Fairchild, "What Does the Bible Say About the Right to Bear Arms?," *Learn Religions*, July 9, 2018, www.thoughtco.com/the-bible-on-the-right-to-bear-arms-701963; "Biblical Self-Defense: What Does the Bible Say about Self-Defense?," www.biblicalselfdefense.com/.

7. Andrew L. Whitehead, Landon Schnabel, and Samuel L. Perry, "Gun Control in the Crosshairs: Christian Nationalism and Opposition to Stricter Gun Laws," *Socius* 4 (2018): 1.

8. F. Carson Mencken, Paul Froese, "Gun Culture in Action," *Social Problems* (January 2017): 1–25, https://doi.org/10.1093/socpro/spx040.

Though guns and Christianity are often associated, this suggests they are actually competing ways of organizing and understanding the world. They are, in effect, two competing religions.[9]

Other chapters in this volume address how the New Testament can inform a faith and worldview that are not reliant on gun violence. But if the willingness to lay down arms and offer self-sacrificial love to one's neighbor, even at the risk of one's own life, is a Christian value, it is one that Jesus found already in the Scriptures he read. The Old Testament has ample resources for peacemaking and disarmament. It turns out to be an important part of Isaiah's message, and part of a broader prophetic emphasis on social justice and the importance of reliance on God instead of on human violence.

This is a theological foray, so it will not be convincing to those for whom the texts have no authority. And it's only a start—there are other, deep issues related to gun ownership that should not be overlooked, such as the strong correlation between progun ideology and racism.[10] But we have to start somewhere.

THE POLITICS OF SELF-DEFENSE

Let's begin with a story. Isaiah 22 contains oracles concerning the times of king Hezekiah of Judah, who reigned in Jerusalem around the end of the eighth century BCE. The

9. Whitehead et al., "Gun Control," 9. The ideology that is actually correlated most strongly is not Christianity itself but "Christian nationalism."

10. Kerry O'Brien, Walter Forrest, Dermot Lynott, and Michael Daly, "Racism, Gun Ownership and Gun Control: Biased Attitudes in US Whites May Influence Policy Decisions," PLOS Global Public Health, *PLOS ONE* 8 (2013): e77552, https://doi.org/10.1371/journal.pone.0077552.

small nation of Judah found itself caught up in the turmoil
of international politics, surrounded by threatening and
heavily armed enemies massing for battle. The people of
Judah lived in a dangerous neighborhood.

When the prophet tells King Hezekiah that the Lord
"has taken away the covering of Judah" (22:8), he is refer-
ring to how, over the course of the preceding century, the
Neo-Assyrian Empire had conquered all the nations that
had once formed a buffer for Judah, protecting it from
larger, more distant empires. Now, those Aramean city-
states and the northern kingdom of Israel are all gone—and
the Assyrians have wiped out nearly all of Judah's defenses,
converging on Jerusalem.

As this was happening, Hezekiah frantically made
preparations to defend his capital city. It was in that context
that Isaiah proclaimed to the king:

> On that day you looked to the weapons of the House
>   of the Forest,
>   and you saw that there were many breaches in the
>   city of David,
>   and you collected the waters of the lower pool.
> You counted the houses of Jerusalem,
>   and you broke down the houses to fortify the wall.
> You made a reservoir between the two walls
>   for the water of the old pool.
> But you did not look to her [i.e., Jerusalem's] Creator,
>   or consider the one who formed her long ago.
>   Isa. 22:8–11

Although translations often render that last line as "You did
not look to him who did it," as if it meant that God had
carried out these public works, it instead refers to the city of

Jerusalem: "you did not look to the One who created her."[11]
Jerusalem—Zion—was the Lord's holy city. The Lord was
her creator and protector. As long as the Lord protected the
city, she was inviolable; but without him, her "guards keep
watch in vain" (Ps. 127:1). Isaiah is reminding Hezekiah of
something he seems to have forgotten: only the Lord can
ultimately protect the city.

But why the reminder? Hezekiah has reacted to
the looming security crisis with public works intended to
fortify and protect the city. First he looks to "the House
of the Forest," also known as "the House of the Forest of
the Lebanon." In 1 Kings 7:2–3 it is described as a large
hall, "one hundred cubits long, fifty cubits wide, and thirty
cubits high" and named for its "four rows of cedar pillars,
with cedar beams on the pillars." This is where Solomon
kept two hundred large, gilded shields, an ornate throne,
and perhaps even vessels of gold, according to 1 Kings
10:16–21. These descriptions suggest that the House of
the Forest was two things: an armory and a storehouse of
precious goods. This wasn't just a building: It was a symbol
of the kingdom's defense capabilities and of its ability to
fund national defense.

Once Hezekiah had taken stock of the treasury, he did
two things. First, he noted that "there were many breaches
in the city of David" (Isa. 22:9), and so he "counted the
houses of Jerusalem, and . . . broke down the houses to
fortify the wall" (22:10). Second, he "collected the waters
of the lower pool" (22:9) and "made a reservoir between
the two walls for the water of the old pool" (22:11). These
are both critical undertakings for a city threatened by an

11. The Hebrew word is 'ōśêhāh, the verb -ś-h plus a *feminine singular* suffix, not a
plural. The immediate feminine antecedent is the mikveh that Hezekiah built, but the city
is a more plausible antecedent in the broader context.

Assyrian army, expert in siege tactics. For Jerusalem to survive a siege, its walls had to be strong—and the people inside needed enough water to last until the enemy either gave up or was driven off by Judah's allies. (Isaiah's frequent warnings against Egyptian alliances, in 19–20 and 30:1–7, suggest that Judah was probably counting on the Egyptians to come to its aid eventually.)

Both of these public-works projects undertaken by Hezekiah have been archaeologically verified. In the case of the wall, a "Broad Wall" was discovered under what is now the Jewish Quarter of modern Jerusalem. It seems to have been built in the eighth century, as Jerusalem was expanding (see 2 Chr. 32:5). Historians often conclude that the fall of the northern kingdom in 721 BCE led to an influx of refugees to Jerusalem, which necessitated the city's expansion into the *Mishneh*, or "second district" (2 Kgs. 22:14). When Assyria threatened the city, this new neighborhood needed to be brought inside the city walls. Especially interesting is that the wall cuts straight through the foundations of former homes—visitors today can see this for themselves, in one of the exposed sections of the ancient wall. Hezekiah's wall construction thus seems to have been an ancient case of eminent domain, in which families were forced out of their homes in the interest of national security.

Hezekiah's water works are even better known than his wall: "Hezekiah's Tunnel" begins just below the City of David and extends a third of a mile down to the Siloam Pool, giving access to the underground spring that gave Jerusalem life without leaving the city walls. These water works are alluded to in 2 Chronicles 32:3–4, 30 and 2 Kings 20:20, suggesting that they were some of Hezekiah's most famous feats. Thousands of people now tour them every year. But this tunnel was apparently completed in great haste—rather than a steady, even channel, it narrows at the midpoint, right where the diggers from the two sides met, as though they were in a hurry to get it finished.

It's clear why the Jerusalemites undertook all this work on walls and tunnels, first proactively and then in a near panic: The Assyrians were terrifying. They possessed the most powerful military and weaponry in the ancient world, as was known throughout the Near East. They boasted of gruesome war tactics in reports of the kings, and their palace walls were adorned with images of Assyrian soldiers impaling their enemies on pikes around a city and piling their heads in great heaps. Assyrians were the inventors of "shock and awe." Israel and Judah had been in the Assyrians' orbit for a century, so they were hardly strangers to the imperial army and its tactics.

Nevertheless, it was only at the end of the eighth century that these overwhelming Assyrian forces came to end the region's resistance once and for all. Their king, Sennacherib, was probably tired of being troubled by these little kingdoms of the Levant; Hezekiah and the other kings in the region had begun refusing to pay their tax and tribute after Sargon died in 705 BCE—daring his successor to prove his resolve in maintaining the empire. In 701 BCE, he did.

When Sennacherib mustered his army, Judah was one of his chief targets. To Isaiah, the threat posed by the Assyrians seemed almost supernatural; he had to resort to mixed metaphors to capture the terror they inspired:

Here they come—swiftly, speedily!
None of them is weary, none stumbles, none
        slumbers or sleeps,
not a loincloth is loose, not a sandal-thong broken;
their arrows are sharp, all their bows bent,

> their horses' hoofs seem like flint, and their wheels
>   like the whirlwind.
> Their roaring is like a lion, like young lions they roar;
> they growl and seize their prey, they carry it off, and
>   no one can rescue.

Isa. 5:26–29

In the aftermath of the campaign, Sennacherib boasted of having destroyed 46 of Judah's towns and cities. One of these was Lachish, Judah's second city, heavily fortified at the top of a large hill; it held out for some time before it was finally conquered and burned. Sennacherib slaughtered many of the inhabitants and threw about 1,500 of the corpses in a mass pit grave. He would eventually have the story of this conquest carved on the walls of his palace in Assyria, showing survivors being tortured and driven out of the city as prisoners. Such images were repeated frequently in Assyrian art and inscriptions and were meant to send a message to other nations: give up without a fight or suffer the consequences.

UNDERSTANDING ISAIAH'S CONDEMNATION

Assyria, by every measure, was a heavily armed enemy threat. Is it unreasonable, then, what Hezekiah did? Far from it, most would say. He seems to have been very practical: fortify the city, ensure supplies in case of siege. Surely he had a right of self-defense? These works arguably saved the city and formed the basis for Hezekiah's enduring fame.

But here's where things become unpredictable: Isaiah is *angry* at Hezekiah for these acts. He accuses him: "you did not look to her Creator, or consider the one who formed her long ago" (22:11). But why? Hezekiah was doing his job, defending the people—and Isaiah condemned him because a few houses had to be taken out! Isaiah looks pretty unreasonable.

It's tempting to spiritualize the situation—as if it would have been fine with Isaiah if Hezekiah had just taken time out for daily devotions at the Temple in the midst of his projects, as a nod to the city's divine creator and protector. But this would be too superficial: in Isaiah's view, Hezekiah has failed at a more basic level.

Or we could conclude that Isaiah's protest is a failed prophecy—one that Isaiah would have taken back after he saw that the city had survived thanks to Hezekiah's building projects. But this seems unlikely: the prophecy would not have been preserved had it not been seen as vindicated by subsequent events.

To understand Isaiah's anger, it's useful to look at how Hezekiah is portrayed in the final form of the book: very negatively, and precisely for being shortsighted. In Isaiah 39, for example, the prophet is said to have warned Hezekiah: "Days are coming when all that is in your house, and that which your ancestors have stored up until this day, shall be carried to Babylon; nothing shall be left, says the LORD. Some of your own sons who are born to you shall be taken away; they shall be eunuchs in the palace of the king of Babylon" (vv. 6–7). Hezekiah says, as if with a shrug, "there will be peace and security in *my* days" (v. 8, emphasis added). He looks like a selfish dope.

To whom did Hezekiah look that way? He certainly didn't authorize that story about himself. Rather, it was written long after his reign, in the wake of the Babylonian destruction of Jerusalem, and it looks back in hindsight on the consequences of Hezekiah's way of thinking. The

contrast it draws—between what seems useful to the present moment and what will be better in the long run—is
important to the book's reflections on Hezekiah's legacy.

Divinely-ordained justice is another of the book's
central themes, and it also helps to make sense of Isaiah's
reaction to Hezekiah. According to Isaiah, the foreign
oppressors will get what's coming to them, because if
God is in control of history, then justice must be done.
As Isaiah 10:12 says, "When the Lord has finished all his
work on Mount Zion and on Jerusalem, he will punish the
arrogant boasting of the king of Assyria and his haughty
pride."

Historically speaking, though, divine justice took a
lot longer to arrive than the Judahites hoped; Sennacherib
was only killed decades later, in a palace coup, as Isaiah
37:38 reports. Neither the power of vengeance nor the tim-
ing of its arrival was within Judah's control. In retrospect,
the people confess: "all that we have done, *you* have done
for us. . . . We have won no victories on earth" (26:12, 18,
emphases added). The defeat of the oppressor is God's
work.

God, not Hezekiah, is responsible for the city's salvation. And it is to God, not Hezekiah, that the people and
their king are ultimately subject. In the Old Testament, this
relationship is described as a covenant, and it involves certain commitments on both sides. When God makes a covenant, God promises help and sustenance. The people, for
their part, are expected to pursue justice and righteousness
(Isa. 5:7; cf. Gen. 18:19; Deut. 6:25). Hezekiah's actions—
tearing down homes and displacing people—abuse his
power, and so violate the principle of divine justice. Isaiah,
like other eighth-century prophets, condemns such practices vociferously, in the name of God:

The LORD enters into judgment
    with the elders and princes of his people:
It is you who have devoured the vineyard;
    The spoil of the poor is in your houses.
What do you mean by crushing my people,
    by grinding the face of the poor?
                                    Isa. 3:14–15

Isaiah's critique of Hezekiah in Isaiah 22 seems connected to this larger program: it is unlikely that the wealthy saw their houses destroyed to make way for the new wall. In our own times, eminent domain actions disproportionately affect poorer residents, because wealthier ones have more resources and access to defend their property. Despite the differences between life now and life then, there is no reason to think it worked differently in Iron Age Judah.

These wider themes suggest that Isaiah's point was not that Jerusalem should just open its gates and allow the Assyrians to ransack it. His criticism of Hezekiah's policies seems to have functioned at a more macro level: Judah never had to be in this situation at all. It's easy to forget that although Jerusalem survived the Assyrian campaign of 701, thousands of Judah's people and dozens of its towns and cities *didn't*. Furthermore, Judah only got into that disastrous situation because of Hezekiah's decisions. One reason the kings of Judah were able to store up so much wealth and arms in the House of the Forest is that they were simultaneously squeezing the poor and avoiding paying tribute to the Assyrians. As far as we know, Isaiah never told Judah's kings not to pay tribute. If the king and his elites had paid tribute, and if they had distributed Judah's wealth more equitably among its people, they wouldn't have been so offensively rich, and they wouldn't have had the Assyrians on their doorstep. Now that

the Assyrians were looming, Isaiah accuses Hezekiah of sub-
jecting the less wealthy to suffering all over again, by having
their houses torn down and replaced with the wall Hezekiah
wants in order to protect himself against the consequences of
his own bad decisions.

Isaiah's message boils down to this: Hezekiah does
not get to appear heroic for his frantic building projects
when his failure to act justly and wisely caused the problem
in the first place. The book of Isaiah portrays Hezekiah as
sparing the city in the short term by throwing himself on
the Lord's mercy (Isa. 37:15–36), but as an ultimately fool-
ish figure, whose weaknesses endangered his kingdom and
the lives of his people. Indeed, Isaiah 39 lays the responsibility for the fall of Jerusalem, the greatest catastrophe the
nation ever experienced, at Hezekiah's feet.

Isaiah's judgment on Hezekiah is consistent not only
with the book of Isaiah, but with other Old Testament prophetic literature that rejects the use of "practical violence"
to defend the tribe. Isaiah's oracles repeatedly contrast the
perils of relying on the machinations of humankind with the
surety of reliance on the plans of God. He warns the ruling
class that making arms deals with foreign nations will get
them nowhere in Isaiah 31:1:

> Alas for those who go down to Egypt for help,
>   and who rely on horses,
> who trust in chariots because they are many,
>   and in horsemen because they are very strong,
> but do not look to the Holy One of Israel
>   or consult the LORD!

The law of the king in Deuteronomy 17:16 likewise forbids
the king from making such deals. Jeremiah even tells his

countrymen that they should submit to the yoke of Babylon (Jer. 27:12).

Even the so-called oracles against the nations, in their final canonical shaping, appeal to the righteous vengeance of God as the route to justice, rather than to the violence of humans. Some prophets go considerably further, with calls to beat swords into plowshares (Isa. 2:4; Mic. 4:3) and reminders to allow God instead of humans to oversee justice.

These were not popular messages—Isaiah 6:9–12 suggests that no one listened to him, and Jeremiah was arrested on suspicion of treason (Jer. 26). It's no surprise that they're not popular today either.

GUNS AS RELIGION

Having lingered for some time in the Old Testament, it's time to move back to the present day. Isaiah's era and our own have certain things in common, not surprisingly. Justice is elusive. What seems practical in the short term is often not the only or even the best way forward. What can be portrayed as heroic is often anything but. One could think of any number of issues that illustrate how those who govern today in America are taking a similarly shortsighted view of the good, from the environment to economics. But the question at hand is guns.

Most of us can imagine scenarios where we might wish to protect ourselves or our families with a gun, so it is necessary to recognize and name the appeal. We are living in a society that is filled with violence and with fears about our neighbors.

But guns are like a wildfire that becomes more

powerful the bigger it gets. The more people who have guns, the more dangerous our society is. The more dangerous our society is, the more people want guns. The more people believe that they need guns to solve their problems, the more problems guns cause.

Gun ownership as a practical, short-term solution to fear has taken on the stature of idolatry for those who believe in guns' power. In the wake of this country's deadly drumbeat of school shootings, Garry Wills has compared Americans' willingness to let our children die rather than restrict the guns that kill them to ancient Near Eastern parents' sacrifice of their children: guns are "our Moloch," the god to which we offer up our children's very lives.[12] When people claim sacred status for guns, revering them above the lives of their children and their neighbor's children,[13] and when guns shape people and their subcultures, defining their identities and setting people in opposition to one another, they become idols. Like false idols, guns make promises of safety and security that they cannot keep (cf. Isa. 44:17–18).

So not only do I know that a gun in my home is far more likely to kill me or someone I love than it is to protect us from someone trying to harm us, I also know that wielding power over life and death is not the way that God calls me to live. As the introduction to the volume describes, in the United States gun ideology has become a pseudo-religious identity and an alternative to Christianity. To place my trust in guns is to deny my trust in God.

12. Garry Wills, "Our Moloch," *The New York Review of Books*, December 15, 2012, www.nybooks.com/daily/2012/12/15/our-moloch/.

13. James E. Atwood, "9mm Golden Calves," *Sojourners* (January 2013): 10–11.

THE EXAMPLE OF JESUS

Isaiah's advice is to look to God. Christians should therefore look to the whole self-revelation of God in the Bible, including the New Testament. At the most crucial moment for his own personal security, Jesus called for his disciples to lay down their swords (Matt. 26:52). Echoing the prophet's calls to break the cycle of violence, Jesus warns that "all who take the sword will die by the sword." The point was recognized even more widely: Jesus was quoting an earlier Greek proverb.

In the Lukan version of the story, Jesus heals the man his compatriot has struck (Luke 22:51). Jesus chooses healing and submission rather than violent resistance. In the Matthean version, we are told that Jesus declined to summon "more than twelve legions of angels" to protect himself (Matt. 26:53). This scene recalls the temptation in the wilderness at the very beginning of his ministry, reaffirming his refusal to use power even for the sake of saving himself. By his actions, Jesus sets an example that inspired later leaders like Martin Luther King Jr. and Mahatma Gandhi.

To many people, the idea of making themselves vulnerable, especially to the point of risking their lives, is unthinkable. And indeed, we have to be very careful about how we invoke that ideal. It must not be used by those who hold great power in society to force the submission of the less powerful. For example, white Americans should not use Christianity as a rationale for telling disempowered minorities to submit to their own subjugation.

Rather than focusing on well-known examples like King and Gandhi, then, let me instead tell a story that's less famous. In March 1996, in the midst of the Algerian Civil War, seven monks of the Trappist order were kidnapped. Their severed heads were found a couple of months later. At the time an Islamic militant group claimed responsibility, although a French general later claimed they had been killed by the Algerian military. What is clear is that they were living in a dangerous situation, with threats on multiple sides, and they knew it.[14]

What makes the story more than a relatively common wartime atrocity is that one of the monks, Christian de Chergé, had written a testamentary letter in which he anticipated his death, two years before he died. He wrote:

If it should happen one day—and it could be today—
that I become a victim of the terrorism which now
    seems ready to engulf
all the foreigners living in Algeria,
I would like my community, my Church and my
    family
to remember that my life was GIVEN to God and to
    this country. . . .
I have lived long enough to know that I am an
    accomplice in the evil
which seems to prevail so terribly in the world,
even in the evil which might blindly strike me down.
I should like, when the time comes, to have a
    moment of spiritual clarity
which would allow me to beg forgiveness of God
and of my fellow human beings,
and at the same time forgive with all my heart the one
    who would strike me down.

14. The monks' story was made into the 2010 French film *Des Hommes and des Dieux* (Of Gods and Men), directed by Xavier Beauvois (France: Why Not Productions, 2010), film.

He goes on to say that the Algerian Muslims are, in God's eyes, "shining with the glory of Christ"—even the man who might kill him. He closes the letter in this way:

> . . . also you, my last-minute friend, who will not
>   have known what you were doing:
> Yes, I want this THANK YOU and this GOODBYE
>   to be a "GOD-BLESS" for you, too,
> because in God's face I see yours.
> May we meet again as happy thieves in Paradise, if it
>   please God, the Father of us both.[15]

Even without the allusions to the Crucifixion, this is a Christlike example: "Father, forgive them; for they know not what they are doing" (Luke 23:34). Though we live in a poisoned society, we still have options: healing like Jesus, or injecting more poison.

Some will say that nonviolence is unrealistic, and the freedom to eschew violence is essentially an expression of privilege—or madness. Miroslav Volf lived through the awful reality of the Balkan conflicts of the 1990s. Like de Chergé, he emphasized a perspective from beyond this world in his book *Exclusion and Embrace*. Its basic question is what to believe and do about human wrongdoing, especially the violence of war, when the cross breaks the cycle of violence. It culminates in an extended reading of the passage in Revelation in which a rider on a white horse appears, "and in righteousness he judges and makes war" (Rev. 19:11). God has to "wield the sword" to judge evil, he says, but human violence is not a proxy

---

15. Testament of Christian de Chergé, https://ocso.org/history/saints-blesseds-martyrs/testament-of-christian-de-cherge/.

for divine violence. Humans do not wield the sword for God. Because Volf has seen the suffering of unchecked violence in war first-hand, he comes to a complex position: "It may be that consistent nonretaliation and nonviolence will be impossible in the world of violence," but if so, "one should not seek legitimation in the religion that worships the crucified Messiah."[16]

So who gets to decide when the killing of human beings is willed by God? No human gets to make that claim. Because ultimately we would make it before the throne of the One who said, "Take up your cross and follow me" (Matt. 10:38; 16:24; Mark 8:34; Luke 9:23).

"DO NOT BE AFRAID"

Those who entrust their lives to their guns are playing deadly games, just as Hezekiah played the deadly military and political games of his times. The "good guys with guns" are not heroes, any more than Hezekiah was. In many people's eyes they seem reasonable, but as Stanley Hauerwas has argued, "The Christian moral position will always seem unreasonable, based as it is on the virtue of hope."[17] In the eyes of God they are all cowering fearfully in their armed bunkers, like Adam hiding in the garden of Eden.

Fear is the first curse in the Bible, brought about by sin. Adam says to God, "I heard the sound of you in the garden, *and I was afraid* . . . and I hid myself" (Gen 3:10, emphasis added). The novelist Marilynne Robinson has

16. Miroslav Volf, *Exclusion and Embrace* (Nashville: Abingdon, 1996), 306.
17. Stanley Hauerwas, *War and the American Difference: Theological Reflections on Violence and National Identity* (Grand Rapids: Baker Academic, 2011), 129.

written that "contemporary America is full of fear"—but that "fear is not a Christian habit of mind."[18]

How often in the Bible does a divine messenger appear with the words, "Do not be afraid"? This is God's message from the beginning to the end: God's message to Abraham (Gen. 15:1); to Hagar (Gen. 21:17); to Isaac (Gen. 26:24); to Hezekiah (Isa. 37:6); to Joseph (Matt. 1:20); to Mary (Luke 1:30); to the shepherds (Luke 2:10); to Paul (Acts 18:9; 27:24); and to John of Patmos (Rev. 1:17). It was God's message to the Israelites fleeing Egypt (Exod. 14:13; 20:20); to the people suffering in exile (Jer. 40:9) and longing to return home (Isa. 41:10; Zech. 8:13). It is God's message to all believers (Luke 12:7, 32).

Fear drives gun ideology. But the entire Bible echoes with the refrain: "Do not be afraid."

18. Marilynne Robinson, "Fear," *The New York Review of Books*, September 24, 2015, www.nybooks.com/articles/2015/09/24/marilynne-robinson-fear/. See also Stanley Hauerwas, "The Church as God's New Language," in *The Hauerwas Reader*, ed. John Berkman and M. Cartwright (Durham, NC: Duke University Press, 2001); 142.

Chapter 4

ISRAELITE BOWS AND AMERICAN GUNS

T. M. Lemos

The bow was a powerful instrument in the ancient world—not only on the battlefield but as a symbol. Indeed, it sometimes appears in unexpected places. After YHWH, the god of Israel, hears the prayer of the infertile wife Hannah and gives her a son, she praises him with these words: "My heart exults in YHWH; my strength is exalted in my God. My mouth derides my enemies, because I rejoice in your salvation. . . . The bows of warriors are broken, but those who once stumbled equip themselves with strength" (1 Sam. 2:1, 4).[1] This is an unexpected way for a woman to celebrate the long-awaited birth of a child, but this juxtaposition is a telling example of the bow's wide-ranging symbolism, which brings together sexuality and reproduction as well as violence.

The bow's symbolism also ties images of human victims with those of prey animals, such that the very divide between human and animal is breached.

The complex ways in which the bow symbolizes power contribute to its tremendous force. It has this in common with the gun; and, like the gun, bow imagery reflects and perpetuates a certain way of thinking about personhood.

1. All biblical translations are my own unless otherwise noted.

Often, ideas about personhood in ancient Israel involved images and practices of physical violence, domination, and "hypermasculinity." Hypermasculinity is an extreme kind of masculinity sometimes referred to as "toxic masculinity." This idea of personhood, grounded in domination, is something that other parts of the Bible take great pains to reject. This has important implications for the place of the gun in the life of contemporary Christians.

THE BOW

The bow is a very ancient and very widespread weapon, having first come into use between ten and twenty thousand years ago and indigenous to every continent except Australia. In ancient West Asia, it first appears roughly ten to twelve thousand years ago.[2] Evidence for its popularity exists in archaeological, literary, and visual forms. Some have argued that the sling was preferred in this area, but there is evidence for use of both weapons. In the Old Testament, there are only about a dozen references to slings but over a hundred references to bows or arrows, indicating a preference for bows. By comparison: the spear is mentioned almost as many times as the bow; both are mentioned fewer times than the sword. The bow is my focus in this chapter because, like the gun, it is a projectile or ranged weapon used for both hunting and warfare.

The Bow as Symbol

The symbolic significance of the bow in ancient Near Eastern sources is fairly consistent: it is used mainly to symbolize

2. P. R. S. Moorey, *Ancient Mesopotamian Materials and Industries: The Archaeological Evidence* (Winona Lake, IN: Eisenbrauns, 1999), 61; Alan H. Simmons, *The Neolithic Revolution in the Near East: Transforming the Human Landscape* (Tucson: University of Arizona Press, 2011), 50.

military prowess and sexual potency.[3] Cynthia Chapman
has recently undertaken a sophisticated treatment of the
language of warfare in which she shows how Mesopotamian
sources connect the bow with warfare, masculinity, and
sexual potency.[4]

In the Babylonian Epic of Creation (also called Enuma
Elish), for example, Marduk shoots an arrow into the belly
of the goddess Tiamat to slay her, before dismembering her
and building the world out of her body parts. In another
example, a well-known Assyrian relief, the Assyrian king is
pictured pointing a large bow at a subjugated city; the city's
residents are portrayed in positions of supplication and as
denuded, decapitated, and impaled corpses. And in one
of his many royal inscriptions, Sennacherib declares: "I
raged up like a lion, then put on armor and placed a helmet
suitable for combat on my head. In my anger, I rode quickly
in my exalted battle chariot, which lays enemies low. I took
in my hand the mighty bow that the god Assur had granted
to me and I grasped in my hand an arrow that cuts off life."[5]
In these examples, which range from mythology to reliefs
to royal inscriptions, we can clearly see the connection
between bows and military dominance.

Evidence for the bow as a sexual symbol is also
widespread. In one Mesopotamian sexual potency
incantation, we read: "May the quiver not become empty!
May the bow not become slack! Let the battle of my

3. Harry A. Hoffner Jr., "Symbols for Masculinity and Femininity: Their Use in
Ancient Near Eastern Sympathetic Magic Rituals," *Journal of Biblical Literature* 85
(1966): 326–34.

4. Cynthia Chapman, *The Gendered Language of Warfare in the Israelite-Assyrian
Encounter* (Winona Lake, IN: Eisenbrauns, 2004).

5. Sennacherib 18, v 11'b–19', according to the *Royal Inscriptions of Sennacherib,
King of Assyrian (704–681 BC), Part 1*, ed. A. K. Grayson and Jamie R. Novotny (Win-
ona Lake, IN: Eisenbrauns, 2012), http://oracc.museum.upenn.edu/rinap/corpus/.
Brackets removed for readability.

love-making be waged!"[6] Sometimes actual bows were used in such rituals.[7] The book of Sirach indicates that Hellenistic-era Judeans held similar conceptions; Sirach 26 warns readers concerning wayward daughters, saying, "Keep strict watch over a headstrong daughter, or else, when she finds liberty, she will make use of it. . . . As a thirsty traveler opens his mouth and drinks from any water near him, so she will sit in front of every tent peg and open her quiver to the arrow" (26:10, 12).[8] We see in these and related examples that the bow is associated with sexual potency and sexual behavior across different cultures and over many centuries. This connection was widespread, no doubt suggested by the ejaculatory and penetrative qualities of arrows.

The bow's masculine associations—both its military and sexual aspects—seems to explain the frequency with which the ancient sources threaten or depict either the seizure or the breaking of the bows of conquered men.[9] Chapman's analysis is compelling:

> [Assyrian] siege scenes depict the removed or broken bows and the crouching posture of enemy males. The Assyrian king and his army are always depicted with their bows either drawn in active battle or carried upright in scenes of deportation following the battle. The enemies' bows, on the other hand, are copiously depicted strewn all over the battlefield,

6. Robert D. Biggs, Šà.zi.ga, *Ancient Mesopotamian Potency Incantations* (Locust Valley, NY: J. J. Augustin, 1967), 37; see also the incantation on p. 33.

7. Biggs, Šà.zi.ga, 37–38.

8. NRSV. As usual, Sirach demonstrates a questionable understanding of female behavior.

9. Chapman, *Gendered Language*, addresses this topic on pp. 50–58. The evidence from Mesopotamia is not limited to the Neo-Assyrian period; the stele of Naram-Sin is a noteworthy earlier example.

broken, and abandoned next to corpses. One scene shows a defeated soldier handing over his bow to an Assyrian soldier. Another shows an Assyrian soldier forcing an enemy officer to cut his own bow. . . . Through the imposition of curses on surrendering vassals, the Assyrian king discredited a male rival through images of feminization.[10]

The Bow and Animalization

The bow was used in antiquity in both hunting and military contexts. This is important in understanding how the bow *condenses* multiple meanings, transforming them into one of the most important symbols of the metaphor war-is-a-hunt. The metaphor war-is-a-hunt—more broadly, power-is-a-hunt—was pervasive, underlying hundreds of ancient sources describing violence. The root metaphor of power-as-hunt is central to the very conceptualization of violence in this region.[11] Through this metaphor, both nonhuman targets and human ones are described as prey. Those inflicting violence are described as predatory animals, such as lions. Even more striking was the practice of animalizing violence, in which the bodies of human victims are treated like animal bodies— flayed, dismembered, and hung up for display. Conquered humans are at once emasculated and dehumanized. Those who perform this violence assert both their superior claim to manhood and their superior claim to "domination personhood": an understanding of personhood centered in physical dominance, violence, and hypermasculinity. This type of personhood was common

10. Chapman, *Gendered Language*, 58–59.
11. T. M. Lemos, *Violence and Personhood in Ancient Israel and Comparative Contexts* (Oxford: Oxford University Press, 2017), 28–59.

throughout ancient West Asia, including ancient Israel. In this context, the bow symbolizes not simply military prowess or sexual prowess or skill in hunting, but all of these. It becomes an exemplary symbol of domination personhood.

Bows were symbols of power in the Bible (1 Sam. 2:3 and Pss. 37:15; 46:9). A striking number of the biblical references to the bow juxtapose hunting imagery, animal imagery, and the language of violence. A noteworthy example is Jeremiah 50, where conquering nations wield bow, spear, and sword against Israel and against Babylon. The chapter contains several overt references to hunting or animal slaughter, five references to bows and arrows, and fifteen references to animals, not to mention various instances of violence against humans. Thus we are told that "A scattered sheep is Israel, driven away by lions. First the king of Assyria devoured it, and now at the end King Nebuchadrezzar of Babylon has gnawed its bones. . . . Surely, the smallest of the flock will be dragged away; surely, their pasture will be appalled over them" (50:17, 45). Conceptions of masculinity as fearsome and dominating and femininity as weak and subordinated appear later in the middle of the chapter, recalling similarly worded curses from extrabiblical sources: "A sword against the Chaldeans—oracle of YHWH—and against the inhabitants of Babylon, and against her princes and her wise men! . . . A sword against her warriors, so that they are terrified! A sword against their horses and against their chariotry, and against all the mixed multitude in the midst of her, so that they become women!" (50:35–37). Jeremiah 51 includes references to bows, slaughtered animals, slaughtered humans, masculine dominance, and subjugation characterized as feminine. Together these chapters exemplify the complex of ideas symbolized by the bow, in which predation, animalization, extreme violence, and masculinity are joined together.

The juxtaposition of bow, hunted animal, and hunted human occurs elsewhere in the Hebrew Bible as well. Other examples include Psalm 11 and Isaiah 5, where we read: "He will raise a standard for nations far away, and whistle for one at the ends of the earth. Here they come, swiftly, rapidly! . . . Their arrows are sharp, all their bows are bent, their horses' hooves seem like flint, and their wheels like the whirlwind. Their roaring is like a lion, like young lions they roar. They growl and seize prey; they carry it off, and there is no one to save it" (Isa. 5:26, 28–29). Isaiah 13:14 describes human victims as "like a hunted gazelle, or like sheep with no one to gather them." A few verses later we read how the Medes will use their bows to slaughter young men, showing no mercy even to children (13:18). The chapter closes with several other animal references. Hunting humans as one would hunt animals is depicted also in Lamentations 3:10, 52 and Amos 2. In Zechariah 9, the image of the bow appears alongside one of drinking human blood. Arrow imagery, animal imagery, and violence against humans also appear together in the oracle of Balaam in Numbers 24; Deuteronomy 32; Psalms 57; 91; Ezekiel 5; 39; and Job 6.

Hosea 2:18 is a particularly interesting case. YHWH states: "I will cut for them a covenant on that day with the beasts of the field, the birds of the heavens, and the creeping things of the ground. The bow, the sword, and war I will abolish from the land; and I will make them lie down in safety." Here we see the bow joined with animal imagery even as YHWH promises to bring violence to an end.

It seems likely that the use of the bow in *both* hunting and military contexts facilitated the conceptual blending of hunting animals and killing humans into the metaphor war-is-a-hunt. The dual use of the bow as an animal-killing weapon and a human-killing weapon abetted the blending of images of hunting with conceptions of violence, such that violence against humans could more easily involve animalizing, dehumanizing elements. Because metaphors are not just figurative embellishments—a kind of mental jewelry—but actually shape our thought and language, this shaped not merely how violence was symbolized but also how it was performed.

While the use of the bow was not solely responsible for the presence or frequency of dehumanizing violence in ancient West Asia, it does seem that the bow had a role to play in the perpetuation and widespread nature of the violence-animalization-hypermasculinity complex that is domination personhood, when we consider the symbolic prominence of the bow and the dehumanizing violence associated with it.

THE GUN AS A POTENT KILLING MACHINE

The comparisons between the bow in ancient West Asia and the gun in contemporary America have already begun to suggest themselves. The parallels are many, though the correspondence is not always precise. Like the bow, the firearm is one of the primary weapons of modern militaries and modern hunters. Like the bow, the gun is widely used in killing both humans and animals.

Hunting remains a significant part of American culture. A 2016 report issued by the United States Department of the Interior reported that 11.5 million people hunted that year. Although this represented a decline of two million from previous years, and only 3.5 percent of the U.S. population, the practice of hunting and images of hunting continue to occupy an important place in the American consciousness.

This is particularly the case in certain regions and among certain subgroups. While only about 1 percent of people in my home state of Rhode Island are paid hunting-license holders, the number for South Dakota is around 26 percent, for Montana 25 percent, and Wyoming 22 percent. The number for Texas is only about 5 percent—but that amounts to over a million people.[12] It seems fair to conclude that the processing of the bodies of hunted animals for consumption remains common, and was even more so in years and decades past.

If this is the case, it also seems fair to examine whether the relative commonness of hunting activities contributes to slippage in imagery between animal killing and human killing in the minds of Americans, as was the case with the bow in ancient West Asia. In fact, examples of such slippage are legion. They appear in literature, film, television, and—unfortunately—in cases of actual violence. In Richard Connell's short story "The Most Dangerous Game," first published in 1924, an American named Sanger Rainsford is traveling to the Amazon to hunt big game and gets marooned on an island. There, he is himself hunted by a Russian aristocrat named Zaroff. This story, of hunter becoming hunted, inspired episodes of quite a few television shows—*Wild Wild West, Gilligan's Island, Bonanza, Fantasy Island, The Simpsons, The Incredible Hulk, Criminal Minds, Law and Order: SVU, The Blacklist, Game of Thrones*, and quite a few others. It has also inspired the films *Predator, The Running Man*, and

12. I am assuming that hunting licenses are a somewhat accurate reflection of partici-pation, and I am counting here only the number of license holders per state, not the total number of licenses, tags, permits, or stamps, which in many cases is far higher. The 2018 numbers from the U.S. Fish and Wildlife Service may be found here: https://wsfrprograms .fws.gov/subpages/licenseinfo/Natl%20Hunting%20License%20Report%202018.pdf.

Hunger Games.[13] More disturbingly, a serial killer active in Northern California in the 1960s and 1970s, the "Zodiac Killer," quoted from Rainsford's story in a letter sent to Bay Area newspapers. While it is less clear whether Robert Hansen—a serial killer active in Alaska in the 1980s—was directly inspired by the story, his kidnapping and hunting of women with a knife and rifle bears similarities. The inventors of paintball were also inspired by the story, as well as by a desire to recreate the rush of hunting buffalo in Africa as a game involving the pursuit of humans.[14]

Examples inspired more directly by the realities of hunting and violence include *The Deer Hunter* and *Apocalypse Now*. Mel Bernstein, the major firearms dealer called "Dragon Man," refers to the weapons he sells as "people-hunting guns."[15] In both ancient Mesopotamian and biblical sources, we see the hunting of animals as prey melding into the hunting of humans as prey, with the bow as the symbolic focus. The same symbolic slippage is mirrored in American culture with the gun as the symbolic focus.

Is the gun a symbol of masculinity and virility like the bow was? In assessing this possibility, it is hard to ignore the gun's nature as a *projectile* weapon or its shape. In *Masculinities*, R. W. Connell writes, "It is a cliché that the gun is a penis-symbol as well as a weapon. Gun organizations are conventionally masculine in cultural style. . . . The gun lobby hardly has to labour the inference that politicians taking away

13. For a long list of television show episodes, films, and other works inspired by this short story, see https://en.m.wikipedia.org/wiki/The_Most_Dangerous_Game. In some of these cases, it may be more a matter of similarity than direct inspiration, but this matters little for the present argument.

14. These examples are also from the Wiki article cited in the preceding footnote.

15. See Michael Paterniti, "Dragonman, the Man Who Sells 'People-Hunting Guns,'" *GQ*, March 7, 2018, https://www.gq.com/story/dragonman-mel-bernstein -sells-people-hunting-guns.

our guns are emasculating us."[16] Despite gun organizations'
outreach efforts to women in recent years, Connell's
assessment stands—the world of guns is a masculinist world
centered around animal killing and military imagery. The
masculine symbolism is reflected and reinforced by gun-
shaped sex toys and novelty items such as penis-shaped
water guns. These crude toys show the connection in the
minds of at least some people between guns and penises.
The masculine dominance of the world of guns is further
exemplified by the fact that in 2015 only 12 percent of
women reported being gun owners, versus 32 percent of
men.[17] Invocations of self-defense, which always involve
the potential for shooting and killing humans, are also—not
coincidentally—extremely racialized.

The correspondence in the symbolism of the bow and
the gun should by now be clear. Both are associated with
masculinity and virility, with military activities, with hunting, and not least of all with a slippage—indeed they facilitate
that slippage—between animal killing and human killing.
Both are associated with the dehumanization of human victims, as the process of killing humans is equated with animal
killing and human victims are equated with prey.

THE GOSPELS' REPUDIATION
OF DOMINATION PERSONHOOD

The symbolic similarity between the gun and the bow matters for Christians. This is not because the New Testament

---

16. R. W. Connell, *Masculinities,* 2nd ed. (Berkeley: University of California, 2005),
212. The book was first published in 1995.

17. See Deborah Azrael, et al., "The Stock and Flow of U.S. Firearms: Results from
the 2015 National Firearms Survey," *RSF: Russell Sage Foundation Journal of the Social
Sciences* 3 (2017): 39.

has a lot to say about bows—it doesn't. The significance of these correspondences requires a broader view.

So, then, what does the New Testament have to say about domination personhood? To be even more direct: What does Jesus have to say about it? What do the incarnation, the crucifixion, and the resurrection say about domination personhood?

One of the primary messages of the Gospels is the refutation of the idea that status should be based on violence, hypermasculine domination, and the dehumanization of subordinated people. One of the main theological points of the crucifixion is to refute this conception of status. Jesus was not a human king; he was not a warrior; he was not even a member of a conquering group. Instead, he was a member of a group of people who had been conquered again and again and again in antiquity. He did not rise up and slay his attackers. He did not place his hand on the neck of his enemies, as Genesis 49 promised Judah would do. He was not a roaring lion seeking prey. He was not fearsome. No. He was tortured; his body was penetrated, impaled, and hung up naked for display—just as the bodies of the victims of the Assyrians were.

The Israelites, who were so often on the receiving end of dehumanizing violence, sometimes critique domination personhood. More often, they yearn and pray to stand in the position of dominators. They ache for vengeance and seek their predatory moment of glory and their hour of traipsing through the blood of others. This is not the vision that Jesus Christ fulfilled—quite the contrary. His crucifixion refutes, in the most dramatic way possible, the conception that divine favor rests with those who make prey of other human beings.

It is remarkable that so many Christians seem not to

see this. Even the writer of Revelation, a book that back-slides so garishly into longings for dehumanizing power—for riding through rivers of human blood (14:20), just as Assyrian kings boasted of doing—even that writer did not see this. Of course, if one understands Revelation as holding equal authority to the Gospels, one could find the grounds to justify not just domination personhood but its most potent symbols, whether bow or gun. However, this seems a tenuous theological position. If there are two radically different strands present in the New Testament on the issue of violence and dehumanization, why would we not err on the side of following Jesus's own words and the example of his own death? Why would we choose the gun, a symbol and an instrument of violence, over the cross, the instrument of torture through which Jesus Christ was emasculated, slain in the most debased of ways?

To hold fast both to guns and to the cross is a contradiction. While human life is rife with inconsistencies, we must ask ourselves openly and honestly whether this most glaring of contradictions is worthwhile. Indeed, we must ask whether it is even possible—or whether the gun and its violence will overwhelm the cross, the weight of which is far too heavy to allow us to carry anything else while we are holding it.

If we are afraid of what losing guns would take from us—masculine dominance, a sense of authorship and agency in a world of violence—we need only look to the model provided by Jesus, a man who lost his masculine dominance along with his bodily integrity. While Jesus may not have been a lion roaring for prey, we well know the author of his life. Domination personhood reduces both aggressors and victims to an identity based on violence; Jesus's life presents us with a symbolism far more powerful than the narratives of domination personhood.

The Gospels present us with a far broader horizon of possibility for human life, but this depends on rejecting the stifling effects of domination personhood. Either we think human beings were created in the image of God—each and every one—or we think some humans are predators and others are prey—that some have value, while others are meant only for slaughter. We can't have it both ways. On this matter, the crucified God we claim to worship gave us clear direction, not just through his words but through the example of his own broken body.

A DIFFERENT ENDING

Ending there would be a bit too easy. There are harder, more personal questions to ask. With this in mind, I end on a note of personal confession.

In the highly polarized political and social environment of the United States, it is easy to focus on a sense of superiority toward those with whom we disagree and on their failure to do as we think they should. This is particularly the case when it comes to disagreements about firearms and gun control.

Writing this essay has made me consider the inconsistencies and symbolic grey zones regarding hypermasculinity and domination personhood in my own life. The working-class Portuguese culture in which I grew up valorized—and continues to valorize—hypermasculinity and the maintenance of social hierarchies based on physical dominance or even physical violence. Even though I consider myself a leftist and a feminist, there are still ways in which I admire certain aspects and symbols of hypermasculinity and domination personhood, in a fashion that perhaps shows an unwillingness on my part to fully embrace the message of Christ's self-sacrificial death.

An example may be found in my daughter's name: Cyrene. Although it was a Stations of the Cross service on Good Friday that reminded me of Simon of Cyrene's role in the passion of Jesus, and thereby led me to consider the name, what really clinched the choice were ancient sources describing Cyrene daughter of Hypseus, who preferred fighting with bronze javelins and killing wild beasts with a sword to weaving or lunching with friends—the more expected activities for a young woman in Greek culture. Her ferocity and bravery drew the attention of Apollo, beardless god of prophecy and pestilence, who married her and brought her to North Africa, where the great city of Cyrene was built in her name. Inspired by this narrative, I made my daughter a shield as my first gift to her and had a lion tattooed on my arm, together with a quote in Greek from the writer Nonnus that translates to "lion-killing Cyrene."

You will note, dear readers, that I did not get a line from one of the Synoptic Gospels discussing Simon of Cyrene on my arm, or an image of Simon carrying the cross for Jesus.

There are many reasons why I am more drawn to the fearsome aspect of my daughter's name than to the aspect of service. First, it is difficult for me as a feminist to be fully inspired by images of service, when for too long it was a foregone conclusion that women, and especially women of color, occupied servile positions—and a woman of color is precisely what my biracial daughter will grow up to be. Although I want her to be generous and Christlike, I also want her to be brave and decisive and—most important—to lead a life free from subordination. This desire comes not just out of my own failing to embrace the truth of the cross but also by the knowledge that the weight of that cross is borne differently by different people in this culture, society, and world of inequality. That is why I am more drawn to Cyrene, wielder of javelin and sword, symbols of strength, than I am to Simon of Cyrene, bearer of the cross, symbol of weakness.

Understandable though this may be, still I must ask myself: Am I strong enough to rid myself of my symbols of strength? Am I assured enough to do this, in order to more perfectly worship a god who clothed himself in human weakness? When I—when we—fail in this task, what is the price of this failure for different groups of people, for those who are oppressed and for those who benefit from structures, symbolic or otherwise, that depend on the oppression of others? The repudiation of domination personhood has different implications for different people, and this is a reality that cannot be ignored as we formulate a "Christian" ethics of violence.

Choosing my daughter's name was an acknowledgment of a tension—in my identity, yes, but also one present in the biblical corpus itself: between a desire to lay claim to the bows aimed at us, in order that we too might have power, and the knowledge that it is only by eliminating domination personhood itself that we can ever truly be free.

The bows of the Israelites are artifacts of a history of subjugation and trauma. However, when artifacts are not just artifacts but sustain momentum to a continuing history of trauma still glaringly active in the world, then they must be eliminated. Whether or not we are too weak to fulfill this, too steeped in the tensions, complexities, and contradictions of human life, the task that Christ calls on us to perform is to lay down our javelins and our rifles, our bows and our handguns, to take up the cross—because it is only the cross, and not the bow or the gun, that makes resurrection possible, for him and for the entire world.

Chapter 5

THIS SWORD IS DOUBLE-EDGED: A FEMINIST APPROACH TO THE BIBLE AND GUN CULTURE

Shelly Matthews

Christians who reach for the Bible to argue for sensible gun control often build their arguments on the New Testament. Does that work? Yes and no. The New Testament has potential to support a peaceful ethic but also contains verses that can be used in support of violence. Only an approach that recognizes the New Testament's double message and chooses its peaceful strands over its violent ones can achieve that goal honestly.

Arguments that the New Testament is solely a book of peace and love are often problematic. They commonly include making a strong contrast between the New Testament and the Old. They note that there is a lot of violence in the Old Testament, including violence that seems to be initiated by and approved by God. Next, proponents of gun control based on Christian teaching about the Bible often proceed to argue that the problem of violence is contained within the Old Testament alone. Once they move to the New Testament (the heart of the Christian gospel, so this argument goes), the overarching or essential message is one of turning the other cheek, loving our enemies, and praying for those who persecute us.

This essay argues against the simple view that while

the Old Testament supports violence, the New Testament
supports peace, and thus that sensible gun control measures
can be supported solely by asking "what the New Testament
says" on the topic. I do not think that those of us who favor
pacifism and commonsense gun control legislation can win
the argument about what the Bible says simply by insisting
that nonviolent resistance, peace, love, turning the other
cheek, etc. represent the one true message of the New Testament. This is because the Bible—and even the New Testament when considered alone—contains multiple voices and
perspectives. Some of these may be used in support of pacifism, but others may be used in support of violence.

Feminist biblical scholars recognize the Scriptures
as double-edged, containing both words that can harm and
words that can inspire, heal, and save. Once we move beyond
assuming that the New Testament is *obviously* on "our side"
as we work for sensible gun control, then we may more effectively use it as a source of inspiration in our work.

VIOLENCE IN THE NEW TESTAMENT

It is perilous to argue that the New Testament is only concerned
with peace and love. To be sure, the New Testament includes
profound and challenging messages of love and peace,
including exhortations to turn the other cheek and to love
enemies. Yet, contrary to widespread assumptions, there is a
good deal of violence within the New Testament as well.[1] One
might organize this violence under three categories:[2]

1. See both E. Leigh Gibson and Shelly Matthews, eds., *Violence in the New
Testament: Jesus Followers and Other Jews under Empire* (New York: T&T Clark,
2005); and Shelly Matthews, *Perfect Martyr: The Stoning of Stephen and the Construction
of Christian Identity* (New York: Oxford University Press, 2010).
2. These categories are drawn from my recent Bible Odyssey article, "Violence
in the New Testament" (https://www.bibleodyssey.org/passages/related-articles/
violence-in-the-new-testament).

First, a number of New Testament authors vilify those with whom they disagree—those they consider to be "the Other." Instances of the verbal violence of name-calling include a troubling saying attributed to Jesus, where "the Jews" are called "the children of the devil" (John 8:44).[3] While much of this verbal violence concerns "the Jews," Gentiles are also subject to name-calling that dismisses them as "Other." In Titus 1:12, the entire population of the island of Crete is dismissed as "liars, vicious brutes, lazy gluttons."[4]

Second, New Testament texts often reflect, rather than challenge, the violent household and political structures of the ancient world. The New Testament was written in a context of violent occupation, owing to Roman imperial rule of the ancient Mediterranean. The Roman Empire placed high value on military conquest and on peace maintained through disciplinary force. Hierarchies enforced by threat of violence were operative in all arenas, from the household up to the imperial center. The empire was also a slave culture. The New Testament, even as it may sometimes attempt to resist violence, cannot escape completely from this violent logic. Jesus tells parables in which beatings of household slaves, even killings, are affirmed as disciplinary measures (e.g., Luke 12:45–47: "But if the slave says to himself, 'My master is delayed in coming,' and if he begins to beat the other slaves . . . the master of that slave will come on a day when he does not expect him and at an hour that he does not know, and will cut him in pieces. . . ."). Paul warns the Corinthians that, as their "father," he might return to them "with a rod," that is, an instrument for beating children (1 Cor. 4:21).

3. Among the signage of the white supremacists who descended on Charlottesville, Virginia, in August of 2017 to defend the confederacy and to chant "Jews will not replace us" was a quotation of John 8:44.

4. Translations of the Bible are from the NRSV unless otherwise specified.

Finally, New Testament authors can imagine and celebrate the final judgment as a violent bloodbath. The book of Revelation serves as exhibit A; its gruesome scenes of cosmic battles, plagues, and bloodshed are well known. While Revelation is often treated as an exceptional case, it is more accurate to understand this book as fully at home within New Testament longing for God's violent judgment against nonbelievers in the end times. Paul imagines Christ at the end of time, handing over the kingdom to God, but only *after* "he has destroyed every ruler and every authority and power" (1 Cor. 15:24). Luke's parable of the nobleman's return, often understood as representing Jesus's second coming, calls for his enemies to be brought forward and slaughtered (Luke 19:27).

To summarize, inasmuch as the New Testament addresses enemies and "others" in hostile practices of name-calling; inasmuch as it assumes violent, patriarchal, and imperial models for household and state; inasmuch as it is filled with expressions of longing for end-times that include the desire for the destruction of nonbelievers, we cannot say that the New Testament is solely concerned with peace and love. Those of us who strive to live out the values of peacemaking, who advocate for sensible gun control legislation as part of those values, will not win the day by claiming that the New Testament is on our side alone.

IS JESUS FOR, OR AGAINST, TAKING UP A SWORD?

Even the question of whether Jesus was a pacifist is not so clear cut as we might wish, with both sides in the gun control debate turning to the practice and teaching of Jesus for support. To illustrate this point, I introduce a pair of verses in Luke that have been interpreted by many biblical scholars in the twentieth century as indications of Jesus' pacifism but by progun forces as justification for unregulated gun ownership.

Two sayings of Jesus in Luke 22 concern swords: one when he shares the Last Supper with his apostles, and another during his arrest on the Mount of Olives. We first take up the passage concerning Jesus' arrest, because it is often used as the basis for interpreting the saying at the supper. The NRSV translates:

> When those who were around him saw what was coming, they asked, "Lord, should we strike with the sword?" Then one of them struck the slave of the high priest and cut off his right ear. But Jesus said, "No more of this!" and he touched his ear and healed him. (Luke 22:49–51)

Since the work of the translating committee for the Revised Standard Version in the 1940s, this has commonly been interpreted in the English-speaking world as showcasing the pacifist Jesus. The disciples are understood to be militant but misguided, in that they use their swords for violent purposes, cutting off the slave's ear. Jesus rebukes them for this violence with the words, "No more of this!" He heals the slave as a means of countering the violent disciples.

It may be, however, that a *desire* for Jesus to be pacifist led to the RSV's interpretation of this passage.[5] D. L. Matson argues that the key Greek verb has been misunderstood, and that the phrase should not be translated as "No more of this," but rather "Permit this to happen."[6] Jesus's words are not a

---

5. David Lertis Matson, "Pacifist Jesus? The (Mis)Translation of ἐᾶτε ἕως τούτου in Luke 22:51," *Journal of Biblical Literature* 134 (2015): 157–76.

6. The phrase is ἐᾶτε ἕως τούτου in Greek. Matson argues that the verb ἐάω is not a verb of prohibition but rather permission.

rebuke of the disciples for their violence but a command that the arrest should be permitted to go forward—the disciples should not do anything to impede the arrest of Jesus. Jesus' healing of the slave of the high priest is a demonstration that he is in control of the current situation, rather than a reprimand of the disciples' violence.

Matson points out that English translations of this phrase had for centuries recognized the sense of the Greek word ἐάω as "permission." Jesus is thus understood as commanding that his arrest not be hindered. Matson shows that the English translation of this text shifted from Jesus exhorting from something to be permitted (the arrest) to something to be prohibited (the violence of cutting off the slave's ear) precisely during the years of World War II, between 1940 and 1942. As Matson describes the process:

> The third draft of the Gospel of Luke, dated to August 1940 and edited by James Moffatt acting as executive secretary of the New Testament revision committee, shows the committee's original revision of the passage ("Let this go no further") . . . crossed out in pencil and a handwritten translation written directly above it: "No more of this!" The date of the change inscribed in the margin of the draft is May 28, 1942. [7]

In the months immediately preceding this penciled amendment, the United States had entered World War II. Matson proposes that the heavy weight of this political event upon the shoulders of the translating committee may have influenced their decision—at least partially, or

---

7. Matson, "Pacifist Jesus?" 169–70.

possibly subconsciously—to take Jesus's words in a more pacifist direction.[8]

The second passage from Luke often brought into arguments concerning Jesus and pacifism is Luke 22:35–38. Many biblical scholars interpret in the direction of pacifism, while those who resist gun control interpret the passage as a justification for their own position. Here, during the Last Supper preceding the arrest, Jesus directs any of his disciples who do not have a sword to sell their cloaks in order to buy one. The disciples respond that they happen to have two swords among them. The passage, in the NRSV, reads,

> [Jesus] said to them, "When I sent you out without a purse, bag, or sandals, did you lack anything?" They said, "No, not a thing." He said to them, "But now, the one who has a purse must take it, and likewise a bag. And the one who has no sword must sell his cloak and buy one. . . . They said, "Lord, look, here are two swords." He replied, "It is enough."

Those who argue that Jesus advocates for his followers to take up weapons see a direct endorsement of their view here. The Gun Owners of America cite this passage as an instance of the New Testament promoting the bearing of arms for self-defense on their website. They argue that the sword Jesus commands his disciples to take up "was the

---

8. The translating committee might also have been influenced by the version of the saying in Matthew, where Jesus' words are more easily read as a direct rebuke of violence. In Matthew, Jesus speaks directly to the one who has cut off the ear of the slave, saying, "Put your sword back in its place; for all who take the sword will perish by the sword" (Matt. 26:52).

finest offensive weapon available to an individual soldier—
the equivalent then of a military rifle today."[9]

Biblical scholars who promote the image of Jesus as
thoroughly nonviolent argue that the reading of progun
advocates is a misreading. They argue that Jesus did not
command the disciples to pick up literal swords but was
speaking metaphorically about strengthening oneself for
the trials ahead. As proof that Jesus was speaking metaphorically, they argue that "it is enough" is Jesus' rebuke of
the disciples for misunderstanding his metaphorical words
as literal ones. As proof that Jesus cannot have literally com-
manded disciples without swords to go out and buy them,
they point to the pacifistic translation of Luke 22:51 just
discussed—"No more of this!" The understanding that
Jesus rebuked the disciples for violence in Luke 22:51
becomes proof that the swords of Luke 22:35–38 are not
real swords.

This pacifist understanding of Luke 22:35–38 is suggested by the footnotes to this passage in the *New Oxford
Annotated Bible*. The annotation for Jesus' exhortation to
"buy a sword" at v. 36 reads:

> An example of Jesus' fondness for striking metaphors
> . . . but the disciples take it literally. The *sword* appar-
> ently meant to Jesus a preparation to live by one's
> own resources against hostility. The natural mean-
> ing of v. 38 is that the disciples suppose he spoke of
> an actual sword, only to learn that two swords were

9. Larry Pratt, "What Does the Bible Say about Gun Control," *Gun Owners of America*, August 1, 1999, https://gunowners.org/fs9902/.

sufficient for the whole enterprise, i.e. were not to be used at all.[10]

To summarize, biblical scholars invested in the image of a nonviolent Jesus—the one who turns the other cheek and teaches enemy love as the highest command-ment—have wanted to argue against the plain sense of the words in this text, the command to buy a sword. Although this passage appears to counsel violence—or, at the very least, to counsel arming at least two disciples with swords—they propose that the text means just the opposite: Jesus' command to buy a sword is metaphorical, and Jesus does not affirm the importance of the swords possessed by the disciples. Rather, he rebukes them for thinking that they should, literally, carry swords. By contrast, those in favor of unregulated access to guns argue that Jesus in the passage literally commands his disciples (and by extension, all of his followers) to take up weapons for the inevitable battles to come.

In short, Christians who promote gun control embrace metaphorical interpretations and broad principles to interpret these passages on Jesus and swords. Propo-nents of unregulated gun ownership assume that a literal reading of the Bible is on their side. Both groups point to the very same verses to support their opposing views. Lis-tening to this debate, I begin to feel as if I have gone back to nineteenth-century debates concerning the Bible and slavery.

10. *The New Oxford Annotated Bible: New Revised Standard Version* (New York: Oxford University Press, 1991), NT 117.

THE USE OF THE BIBLE IN NINETEENTH-CENTURY
AMERICAN ARGUMENTS OVER SLAVERY

The political and religious arguments of the nineteenth century over whether or not American slaveholding practices were just or unjust illustrate the problem of Christian attempts to align moral precepts and ethical practices to "what the Bible says."[11] As the historian J. Albert Harrill points out, if the question were merely how the results of scientific, literal exegesis of the Bible should shape Christian ethics, the slaveholders win. Abolitionists had a more difficult time than slaveholders did building arguments against slavery from a scientific and literal reading of the Bible. For example, some who attempted to defend antislavery positions proposed that there were no slaves in the New Testament, only servants. This argument was built on the shaky ground of claims that the Greek word *doulos* meant "servant," not slave—an argument easily refuted by critical philology.

Because it was difficult to defend antislavery positions based on literal readings of the Bible, abolitionists were forced instead to tease out broad interpretive principles. They pointed to the so-called Golden Rule, arguing that a principle as lofty as "do onto others as you would have them do onto you" made it impossible to own slaves. Or they argued that the antislavery ethics of the Bible were so deeply embedded that they were actually hidden from sight for the first readers of the Bible, only coming to light

11. See especially J. Albert Harrill, "The Use of the New Testament in the American Slave Controversy: A Case History in the Hermeneutical Tension between Biblical Criticism and Christian Moral Debate," *Religion and American Culture: A Journal of Interpretation* 10 (2000): 149–86; and Sylvester A. Johnson, "The Bible, Slavery and the Problem of Authority," in *Beyond Slavery: Overcoming Its Religious and Sexual Legacies*, ed. Bernadette J. Brooten (New York: Palgrave Macmillan, 2010), 231–48.

for the more enlightened readers of the current abolitionist movement, centuries later.[12]

Slaveholders and proponents of slavery, on the other hand, could simply point to what they considered the plain sense of the text. Both testaments of the Christian Bible were written in slaveholding cultures, and both contain numerous verses that assume the normalcy of slaveholding, as well as numerous exhortations that can be literally read as supporting slaveholding practices. With respect to the New Testament, they drew sanction for slavery especially from passages concerning the submission of slaves to their masters (Col. 3:18–4:1; Eph. 5:22–6:9; and 1 Pet. 2:18–3:7).[13]

Now we can all concede, without qualification, that slavery is unjust. Those of us who are Christian can say, without qualification, that the God we worship and seek to know better does not countenance slaveholding. We know with certainty that the Jesus Christ we seek to emulate stands in solidarity with slaves and condemns slaveholding practices. Our conscience guides us to this position; our desire for justice and human flourishing guides us to this position—despite individual proslavery passages in the pages of Scripture.

Whether the question is the Bible and slavery, the Bible and sexuality, or the Bible and guns, we cannot

12. See Harrill's discussion of the "seed growing secretly" interpretation of Col. 4:1 ("New Testament American Slave Controversy," 154–57). Abolitionists argued that the exhortation for masters to treat their slaves "justly and fairly" was really an exhortation to abolish slavery, since the only just and fair treatment of slaves was to set them free. They argued that while first readers of Colossians did not understand the verse as antislavery, the author planted in it the seed of abolition, which would grow "secretly," and eventually into the full-blown antislave-holding stance of the nineteenth century.

13. Because these passages in Colossians, Ephesians, and 1 Peter outline the authors' views of how subordinate members of the household—wives, slaves, and children—are to submit to the head of the household in his respective roles as husband, master, and father, they are often referred to in scholarly discussions as "The Household Codes."

rest our claim on establishing what the Bible "really" or "literally" says. Questions about how to place biblical teaching with respect to modern justice debates cannot be answered simply by relying on biblical criticism to peel away misconceptions and misinterpretations and pull out the kernel of pristine ethical truth. The Bible is multilayered and multivoiced; it can be used in support of justice but also in support of injustice. This is clear with respect to slavery and holds also for the issue of sensible gun control legislation.[14] Questioning the use of the Bible to uphold unjust social practices, while controversial in some circles, is part and parcel of the feminist biblical interpretation with which I identify and which we now turn to consider.

A DOUBLE-EDGED INTERPRETIVE SWORD

Rather than arguing that the Bible supports my view on gun control, and not the views of those who embrace unrestricted sale and possession of military-grade assault rifles, my feminist commitments and values lead me to take a different tack. A key aspect of feminist biblical interpretation is the observation that the Bible was written in a patriarchal—or *kyriarchal*[15]—context and that these aspects of the Bible must be identified, critiqued, and rejected for the sake of our salvation. This is especially crucial for those who have

---

14. Consider here also Johnson, "Bible, Slavery, Problem of Authority," 244–45.

15. The word *patriarchy* is built from the Greek words for "father" and "rule." Because not all men rule, and because human beings are variously situated with respect to power and ruling—based not just on their gender but also on race, class, sexuality, nationality, etc.—Schüssler Fiorenza suggests that patriarchy is not the best word to articulate the realities of power and domination. Drawing from the Greek word for master or lord, *kyrios*, she introduced the word "kyriarchy"—"rule of the masters/lords"—as a way to acknowledge that power to rule depends not just on gender privilege but also on other aspects of privilege.

experienced passages from the Bible as oppressive. Simply and directly, while there may be passages supporting violence within the Scriptures, we reject them as resources for ethical behavior.[16]

Yet, though we identify and critique texts that affirm patriarchal or kyriarchal oppression, we do not merely reject the unsavory passages and walk away from the text altogether. As Elisabeth Schüssler Fiorenza observes: at its best, the Bible is a text that "cultivates a dream world without domination, poverty, oppression. . . . This dream inscribed in religious scriptures becomes repeatedly incipient reality here and now through the struggles of sociopolitical-religious liberation movements."[17]

The Bible contains texts that can support the amassing of guns as well as those that can support the dismantling of weapons. These two kinds of texts—the violence-affirming ones and the peace-affirming ones—are not necessarily located in two distinct places, such that we can easily find the verse we want. Sometimes the very same text can be interpreted in either a peaceful or a violence-affirming way. Indeed, liberating texts and oppressive texts are often very near to each other, sometimes even interwoven. There was a perpetual struggle within early Christian communities between voices and perspectives that embraced kyriarchal structures of oppression and those that leaned towards utopian, visionary, democratic practices of justice.[18] The sword of a liberation-minded interpreter is necessarily

16. A famous and analogous instance of cutting out scriptural passages that do harm comes from the theologian Howard Thurman, who tells of his grandmother cutting out passages from the Bible that argued in support of slavery.

17. Elisabeth Schüssler Fiorenza, *Congress of Wo/men: Religion, Gender, and Kyriarchal Power* (Cambridge, MA: Feminist Studies in Religion Books, 2016), 6.

18. See, for instance, Elisabeth Schüssler Fiorenza, *But She Said: Feminist Practices of Biblical Interpretation* (Boston: Beacon, 1992), 81, 94–95.

double-edged: we may assess every biblical passage for both its liberating and its oppressive potential.

Some might object that this is a completely subjective approach to biblical interpretation; that it leaves it all up to individuals to choose whether or not the verses they prefer justify their desire to own a high-power automatic rifle; that by allowing that all biblical passages must be assessed, and that some might be rejected, we are deprived of any basis for our moral knowledge. I would respond that there are broad principles involved in our feminist choices—including community benefit, human flourishing, and the all-important principle of neighbor love. Here, feminist interpretation stands in a principled line with Saint Augustine, who also relied on such a standard when he wrote: "If it seems to anyone that they have understood the divine scriptures, or any part of them, in such a way that by that understanding they do not build up that double love of God and neighbor, they have not yet understood."[19]

FIRST TIMOTHY: PROVIDING FOR ONE'S FAMILY AND THE CASTLE DOCTRINE

To illustrate this method of interpretation, I turn to two different strands of thinking on the early Christian household, both from the New Testament. One I reject for its violence; one I offer as a resource for those who work for more just and peaceful households and, by extension, a more just and peaceful society.

Websites promoting unregulated gun ownership based

---

19. Translation modified from Augustine, *De Doctrina Christiana*, ed. R. P. H. Green (Oxford: Clarendon, 1995), 49 (book I, ch. 36, para. 40).

on biblical teaching commonly cite 1 Timothy 5:8: "And whoever does not provide for relatives, and especially for family members, has denied the faith and is worse than an unbeliever." The verse is considered as a progun biblical passage insofar as it justifies the so-called castle doctrine. The castle doctrine supports the use of deadly force to protect the home and its inhabitants. First Timothy's statement that it is necessary for believers to "provide for" their own is understood to mean that the male head of household must keep a gun in the home to defend against intruders.

On the face of it, such an interpretation is a stretch. The larger context of the Timothy passage is the *financial* burden that widows put on the church if they are "enrolled," receiving financial support from the church rather than from their families (1 Tim. 5:3–10). In context, 1 Timothy's exhortation that one should provide for the family suggests financial support rather than protection with a semiautomatic rifle. That said, at least one common thread links this verse from 1 Timothy and the "castle doctrine."

The Greek word *tis*, translated in 1 Timothy 5:8 as "whoever," is not a random whoever. Rather, it designates a specific person within the ancient household: namely, the head of the household—the *paterfamilias*. In the ancient household, this husband/father/master had total authority—even life-and-death authority—over the wives, children, and slaves within the household. Those called "his own" are all the family members and slaves under the control of this head of the house. In a similar way, the castle doctrine assumes that the right to own—and necessity of owning—a gun does not apply to everyone, but is reserved for the patriarch who rules the house. Both the proponents of the castle doctrine and the author of 1 Timothy 5:8 are thinking of the singular role of the male head of household, whether for provision or protection. In positive scenarios, this might be understood as authority to provide, protect, and defend. Unfortunately, this authority can also be used to discipline, punish, or threaten, by whatever means the lord/master/father deems necessary.

As a feminist, I reject the castle doctrine as an expression of toxic masculinity. Guns are used vastly more often in situations of domestic violence than as a form of protection from outside intruders. Most often when a homicide occurs by gun in a household, the head of household kills his wife and/or children.[20] As a feminist biblical scholar, I reject the toxic masculinity of the pastoral epistles, including 1 Timothy, as well as other passages that argue for the submission of all household members to the *paterfamilias*—the kind of deference that paves the way for the castle doctrine.

But, with my double-edged feminist interpretive sword—analyzing for patriarchal/*kyriarchal* oppression, but also for liberating, visionary, and utopian-leaning strands within the text—I ask what other biblical models of the household might inspire the work of peacemaking. Is there a different model of masculinity and a different model of family life, articulated within the New Testament, than one that encourages the head of the household to take up lethal weapons to defend—but potentially also to kill—subordinate family members?

In order to cultivate a world without the toxic masculinity linked to gun violence, I draw on a different cluster of verses from the New Testament—the teachings of Jesus

---

20. For one study documenting this household violence, see Sarah Mervosh, "Gun Ownership Tied to Domestic Homicides, Not Other Killings, Study Finds," *New York Times,* July 23, 2019.

that are sometimes categorized as the antifamily sayings. There are a number of Gospel passages in which Jesus speaks hard sayings about family life: for example, "whoever wants to be my disciple must hate mother and father" (Luke 14:26a); or "I have come to set a man against his father, and a daughter against her mother" (Matt. 10:35). Among these hard sayings are passages that challenge the patriarchal ordering of the culture. Consider this saying, preserved in Matthew, which radically questions the status of earthly fathers: "But you are not to be called rabbi, for you have one teacher, and you are all students. And call no one your father on earth, for you have one Father—the one in heaven. Nor are you to be called instructors, for you have one instructor, the Messiah" (Matt 23:8–10). Or, in a passage from Mark, where fathers are given up when one leaves one's household, and are not among the family members regained: "Truly I tell you, there is no one who has left house or brothers or sisters or mother or father or children or field . . . who will not receive a hundredfold now in this age—houses, brothers and sisters, mothers and children, and fields . . ." (Mark 10:29).

In contrast with 1 Timothy, or the well-known calls to subordination to the husband/master/father in Colossians, Ephesians, and 1 Peter, these Gospel sayings call into question the ideal of a household ruled by a patriarch. Matthew exhorts his hearers to call no one father on earth. Mark promises that those who leave households with fathers, mothers, sisters, brothers, and children will get back all of those family relations—*except* fathers.[21]

---

21. I draw these observations on alternative models of household from Elisabeth Schüssler Fiorenza's landmark work, *In Memory of Her: A Feminist Theological Reconstruction of Christian Origins*, 10th Anniversary Edition (New York: Crossroads, 1993), 145–51.

These anti-father sayings are not anti-men sayings.
Men are included in the ideal household promised in Mark
10: these are houses with brothers, sisters, mothers, and
children. Because this is so, they are not anti-dad sayings;
they do not suggest that men should not have or care for
children. Rather, they hold up a different kind of family
relationship for men: they are called to be *brothers*, rather
than to assume the role of the patriarch possessing the
power and the right to punish and kill.

I hold up this biblical notion of a family with *brothers*
instead of *fathers* as a counter to the biblical notion of the
paterfamilias, who paves the way for the castle doctrine. I
follow here Jane Schaberg, who took the brother figure as
a key to her reflection on the possible historical relationship between Mary Magdalene and Jesus. She writes that
the brother figure was

> particularly helpful . . . in reconceptualizing the
> figure of Jesus, thinking about the participation
> of women in the early Christian movement, and
> thinking about the crucifixion/resurrection materials
> . . . Jesus reconceived as a brother: a male who is not
> a father, not a lover, a male who might be a guide to
> the limited male world, or who might even be guided
> into women's spheres, thus confusing private and
> public. Who might use the power and privilege he
> has to defend and foster, to open doors. Not hero or
> leader or God, but companion . . .[22]

The biblical text encourages us to tease out from this

22. Jane Schaberg, *The Resurrection of Mary Magdalene: Legends, Apocrypha, and the Christian Testament* (New York: Continuum, 2004), 43.

image a larger role for brother-type masculinity in our own households. Could a vision of Jesus as brother—along with the biblical call for household relations where men stand as brothers and children alongside sisters and mothers, within a family where no one is called "Father"—inspire us in the struggle to end gun violence?

Other New Testament texts hint at these alternate households as well: the home of Mary, Martha, and Lazarus in Bethany, where Martha, not Lazarus, presides at the meal (John 12:2-7); the missionary cooperation of the married partners Prisca and Aquila (coteachers of Apollos at Acts 18:26; coworkers of Paul at Rom. 16:3).

In present-day America, ethical practices of men as brothers in alternate households "using their power and privilege . . . to defend and foster, to open doors," might include taking on the role of an ally and advocate, rather than assuming the "natural" place as spokesman for a group working for gun control. It might mean keeping an eye out for bullies, calling them to account and helping them to redirect their behaviors, and also keeping an eye out for those who are bullied, reaching out to them with compassion so that they are not drawn to react to their victimization with acts of revenge.

As a feminist biblical scholar working toward this end, these brothers within alternate households inspire me: not patriarchs who rage and rule with lethal weapon in hand, but comrades and companions committed to the struggle for peace and human flourishing.

Chapter 6

CAN A CHRISTIAN OWN A GUN?

David Lincicum

Can a Christian own a gun? At first blush, the question might seem impossibly stupid: according to a 2017 report by the Pew Research Center, the United States has the highest number of guns per capita (followed at some distance by Serbia). Something like 30 percent of the population own guns, with 42 percent of adults living in a gun-owning household.[1] These numbers already suggest that there are tens of millions of Christian gun owners in the United States. This suspicion is confirmed when studies of religious affiliation are taken into consideration: Protestants constitute the highest percentage of gun owners (with white evangelicals, perhaps predictably, leading the way), more than Catholic, Jewish, or nonreligious populations. As the sociologist David Yamane notes, "[t]he positive relationship between Protestant religious affiliation and gun ownership is one of the best established . . . findings in the literature on gun ownership in America."[2]

---

1. See the report, "America's Complex Relationship with Guns," Pew Research Center, June 2017, http://www.pewsocialtrends.org/2017/06/22/americas-complex -relationship-with-guns/.
2. David Yamane, "Awash in a Sea of Faith and Firearms: Rediscovering the Connection between Religion and Gun Ownership in America," *Journal for the Scientific Study of Religion* 55 (2016): 622–36 (623), https://doi.org/10.1111/jssr.12282. Cf. also Robert L. Young, "The Protestant Heritage and the Spirit of Gun Ownership," *Journal for the Scientific Study of Religion* 28 (1989): 300–309; Sarah Eekhoff Zylstra, "Praise

So, to ask whether a Christian can own a gun might seem like a willfully dense, counterfactual question, like asking whether birds can have wings. But my question is about the "oughtness" of such an action: Can Christians, acting in their capacity *as Christians*, own guns? Or are the moral problems inherent in gun ownership sufficient to render it forbidden? In this chapter, I argue against the ethical appropriateness of Christian gun ownership. For the sake of the current argument, I'm setting aside gun ownership for hunting or sport shooting or collecting and thinking about the gun primarily as a means of self-defense or defense of others. I also set aside those professions (e.g., military or police) that would require one to carry a firearm in public duty. The debate about whether Christians ought to serve in the military is an ancient one but is better left for another context.

It would be possible to take a pragmatic tack in answer to the question "*Should* a Christian own a gun?" and point out the practical risks involved in owning a gun. I could note, for example, the correlation between gun ownership and suicide: according to the Centers for Disease Control (CDC), in 2017 some 23,854 people died by suicide with a firearm in the US.[3] Or I could point out the studies that indicate that someone is up to 4.5 times more likely to be

the Lord and Pass the Ammunition, Quantified," *Christianity Today*, July 24, 2017, https://www.christianitytoday.com/news/2017/july/praise-lord-pass-ammunition-who-loves-god-guns-pew.html.

3. According to the CDC, in 2017 (the latest year for which data is available), 14,542 people died by homicide involving a firearm, with another 23,854 by suicide with a firearm (CDC's WISQARS database, https://webappa.cdc.gov/sasweb/ncipc/leadcause.html). Among the sprawling literature on firearms and fatality, see David A. Brent and Jeffrey Bridge, "Firearms Availability and Suicide: Evidence, Interventions, and Future Directions," *American Behavioral Scientist* 46 (2003): 1192–1210; Linda L. Dahlberg, Robin M. Ikeda, and Marcie-jo Kresnow, "Guns in the Home and Risk of a Violent Death in the Home: Findings from a National Study," *American Journal of Epidemiology* 160 no. 10 (2004): 929–36; Daniel W. Webster and Jon S. Vernick, eds., *Reducing Gun Violence in America: Informing Policy with Evidence and Analysis* (Baltimore: Johns Hopkins University Press, 2013).

shot if he or she owns a gun.[4] But instead of approaching this task merely pragmatically, I intend to look to the New Testament for its theological and moral guidance. After all, Protestants of all people should be interested in deriving moral guidance from the New Testament.

But is the New Testament relevant? It knows nothing of guns, nor does it reflect at length on other means of violence that might have been known in antiquity. It accounts for only 31 of the 473 references in the Bible to the "sword," and these are mostly in narrative or apocalyptic contexts, where questions of normative ethics are not clearly in view. But we can take inspiration from the church's tradition of interrogating the text with our own questions, formulated in the present and derived from our experience. If we pose our contemporary questions about guns to the biblical texts, we will find they are not silent in reply, even though guns are nowhere mentioned in them.

A different sort of issue is posed by the violent passages in the New Testament that might be (and have been) co-opted into the service of further violence: from the strident polemical language of the Gospels of Matthew and John to the pleading hope of Revelation's martyrs that God will avenge their blood on the inhabitants of the earth.[5] To ask the New Testament to be pressed into speaking to our twenty-first-century problem of gun violence might therefore seem initially unpromising. Indeed, an alternative reading of the New Testament, not entirely hypothetical, might unfold along the following lines: Jesus came to offer

---

4. Charles C. Branas, Therese S. Richmond, Dennis P. Culhane, Thomas R. Ten Have, and Douglas J. Wiebe, "Investigating the Link between Gun Possession and Gun Assault," *American Journal of Public Health* 99 (2009): 2034–40

5. For some reflections on these texts, see Shelly Matthews and E. Leigh Gibson, eds., *Violence in the New Testament* (London: T&T Clark, 2005).

a message of personal salvation, not to regulate societal norms. He even encourages his disciples to sell their cloaks in order to buy a sword, presumably for the purpose of self-defense (Luke 22:36).[6] Didn't he sanction the use of a stand-your-ground mentality when he said, "if the owner of the house had known in what part of the night the thief was coming, he would have stayed awake and would not have let his house be broken into" (Matt. 24:43)? Therefore, the New Testament's witness should be understood as condemning aggressive violence but not the regulated use of force in self-defense or defense of others, for which guns are an acceptable means.

I invite you to consider what follows to be a counter-reading. The preceding progun argument is contestable at every point, but rather than contesting it point by point, which would run the risk of conceding that the argument is to be decided by prooftext, I'd like to think about what the gun offers to the individual, and how this squares with the New Testament's understanding of the person's role in the world. More forcefully put, my thesis is simple: the gun is a temptation to arrogate life-destroying power to the wielder and should be resisted by those who follow in allegiance to a crucified Messiah.

To back up this thesis, I present eight sub-theses.

1. Technologies extend the range of moral choices and possible actions available to the user.

Technologies are the result of human craft, and when they are concentrated in discrete physical instruments, they are no longer just inanimate "objects." Bruno Latour writes that

6. For some qualifying thoughts on how to read this text, see François Bovon, *Luke 3: A Commentary on the Gospel of Luke 19:28–24:53,* Hermeneia (Philadelphia: Fortress, 2012), 183.

when a person and a gun interact, there is a mutual trans-
figuration of both subject and object into a new composite:

> You are different with a gun in your hand; the gun is
> different with you holding it. You are another subject
> because you hold the gun; the gun is another object
> because it has entered into a relationship with you. The
> gun is no longer the gun-in-the-armory or the gun-in-
> the-drawer or the gun-in-the-pocket, but the gun-in-
> your-hand, aimed at someone who is screaming.[7]

In other words, to hold a gun is to find oneself faced with
an extended range of possible actions. But if a gun extends
the range of possible actions available to a person, it also
extends the range of possible *moral* actions, and so opens
that person up to new possibilities of moral scrutiny.

*2. A person wielding a gun has an enlarged range of possible
actions before him or her at any time, including the option
to fatally shoot another human. Thus, the choice to carry or
wield a gun should be conceived as a conscious decision to
extend one's moral capacities to include killing instantly.*

Fatality belongs properly to the *telos* of a weapon. That is
to say, a gun is designed for the purpose of killing. To use a
gun to hammer a nail or squash a fly is possible, but the gun
is designed to kill; it achieves its proper purpose when used
to kill. We tend to trade in euphemisms, so we might say
that we'd like to have a gun for safety, for peace of mind, for

---

7. Bruno Latour, *Pandora's Hope: Essays on the Reality of Science Studies* (Cambridge, MA: Harvard University Press, 1999), esp. ch. 6, quote from 179–80. On
the "actant," see p. 303. One might also compare the controversial study by Leonard
Berkowitz and Anthony LePage, "Weapons as Aggression-Eliciting Stimuli," *Journal of
Personality and Social Psychology* 7 (1967): 202–7.

protection, or "just in case." But any serious consideration must clear-sightedly remember precisely what a gun is designed to do and the capacity it gives its user. It would be clearer to say that we desire to own a gun in order to kill instantaneously should the necessary occasion arise. In the 2017 Pew Research Survey, 67% of gun owners cite protection as the most important reason for owning a gun, with more than half of white evangelicals (57%) agreeing. Much smaller percentages prioritized hunting (21%), sport shooting (10%), or their job (1%).[8]

Needless to say, to navigate the world with the capacity for instantaneous lethal force is to navigate the world as a profoundly different type of self than that envisaged by Jesus and his followers. Nowhere, in all its paraenetic material, does the New Testament seriously consider the possibility that those it addresses would be capable of such immediate lethal violence. The technological innovations of the last few centuries have led to possibilities previously unimaginable and so require us to think very carefully about whether the moral entailments of a gun-carrying self can square with the self envisioned by the New Testament.

3. The action of killing instantly, or attempting to do so, can be undertaken with a variety of motives (self-defense, aggression, greed, intervention in a violent conflict) and so can be morally valuated in different ways. But humans act under the influence of passions, basic emotions, and dispositions that incline us toward one course of action or another.

It would be counterproductive and wrongheaded to consider unprovoked murder with a gun as morally equivalent to killing in self-defense. But when violent force might be justified or necessary, even in self-defense, is not at all obvious. Even under normal circumstances, people struggle to make maxi-

---

8. See the analysis in Zylstra, "Praise the Lord and Pass the Ammunition."

mally rational decisions. Their ability to do so very quickly and under the influence of intense emotions is even less. The New Testament envisions humans as subject to self-deception and violent tendencies and does not think of fear or self-defense as a legitimate motive for violence or lethal force. Paul considers humanity under the regime of the flesh to be given to "strife, jealousy, anger, quarrels, dissensions, factions, [and] envy" (Gal. 5:20–21). Even if he believes that "those who belong to Christ Jesus have crucified the flesh with its passions and desires" (Gal. 5:24), Paul is well aware of the ongoing threat of regression and instructs Christians against letting "sin exercise dominion in your mortal bodies, to make you obey their passions" (Rom. 6:12). Even the crucified Christian's members are potential instruments of wickedness. Paul's realistic anthropology calls into question any view of human decision-making that sees us as coolly rational and able to fulfill the role of judge in an untroubled manner, without passion clouding our minds. Rather, Christians taught by Paul should be suspicious of our own motives, our own propensity to rationalize a course of action, and even to justify unnecessary violence as necessary. This pessimistic anthropology considers the person to be prone to violence and so suggests that to strengthen or radicalize the opportunities for such tendencies to take effect would be profoundly worrisome.

4. Above all, the New Testament envisions the Christian life as a via crucis, *a following after the one who was subjected to violent mistreatment and did not resist in return. The call to the* imitatio Christi *means nothing if not this.*

The Gospels are relentless in their depiction of the disciples as those who *follow* Jesus. Mark, for one, is explicit about where this leads: from Galilee where Jesus calls the disciples, along with him, on the Isaianic way, to Jerusalem to die. Mark's Jesus calls readers beyond the text, and beyond the circle of his first followers: "If any want to become my followers, let them deny themselves and take up their cross and follow me. For those who want to save their life will lose it, and those who lose their life for my sake, and for the sake of the gospel, will save it" (Mark 8:34–35). The address is here generalized: if *anyone* wants to follow Jesus, they must be prepared to suffer the way he did—passively, at the hands of those wielding violent power, to death.

Is it possible to imitate Christ while at the same time standing one's ground? Can I exercise my legal right to shoot someone who breaks into my house, killing them for the attempted theft of property or harm to my person, while at the same time imitating the one who "when he was abused, did not return abuse; when he suffered, he did not threaten; but he entrusted himself to the one who judges justly" (1 Pet 2:23)? Would this impulse toward self-defense not be "wanting to save my life"—the very thing that Jesus says will lead to its ultimate loss?

The master narrative of the Christian faith involves Jesus facing those who wished to take his life and renouncing the violent strategies of resistance that might have saved him. This is the narrative that wants to structure Christian practice in the world—rather than the counternarrative that enshrines a violent hero who overthrows the evildoers with a superior display of marksmanship: the famous "good guy with a gun" story, so alien to basic Christian sensibilities but so familiar to American ears.

5. The Gospels depict Jesus himself as prohibiting acts of violence even in self-defense and speaking against being seized by the fear of death, which he considered only a penultimate reality.

"Do not resist an evildoer" (Matt. 5:39) is one of the Sermon on the Mount's pronouncements that the church has been squirming under for two thousand years. But the command is clear. It is not supplied with exception clauses ("unless they are attempting to take something that is yours"), and the call to nonviolent resistance is striking. As one of the earliest commentators on Matthew wrote: "For if you strike back, you have denied that you are Christ's disciple, not with words but with deeds."[9]

The strictest interpretation of this saying—that it commands nonviolence and prohibits all retaliation—has not often been pursued since Constantine conquered under a Christian banner. But that is not sufficient to defuse the force of the command.[10] Even if we would suggest to Jesus that he make some exceptions, the command goads us repeatedly; it challenges us to become a "sign of contrast" to the broader world in which Christians live.[11] As Ulrich Luz says, this is an "expression of a protest against dehumanizing spirals of violence and of the hope for a different kind of personal behavior than what can be experienced in everyday life."[12]

Indeed, when offered the opportunity to sanction acts of violence in defense of himself at his arrest, Jesus declines, and instructs his disciples not to pursue force. Nor does Jesus indicate that fear of death is an acceptable motive for violence; rather, he urges, "Do not fear those who kill the body but cannot kill the soul; rather fear him who can destroy both soul and body in hell" (Matt. 10:28). Paul, moreover, urges doing good to one's enemies (Rom. 12:20).

We live in a world that is increasingly violent, in which political manifestos are underlined with mass

9. *Opus imperfectum in Matthaeum* 12, as cited in Ulrich Luz, *Matthew 1–7: A Commentary*, Hermeneia (Minneapolis: Fortress, 2007), 277.

10. Cf. Luz, *Matthew 1–7*, 277–82.

11. The phrase "sign of contrast" is Luz's: see *Matthew 1–7*, 281.

12. Luz, *Matthew 1–7*, 274.

shootings, and petty squabbles are resolved with bullets. In such a context, would embracing nonviolent resistance be to lay down before the lion and to acquiesce? To cede ground to evil? To disarm the "good guys" so that the "bad guys" can have their way? Real political questions like those are important, but the example of Jesus and the teaching of Paul urge us toward *Christian difference*—toward an embodied protest that might call the followers of Jesus to be, like him, an innocent sufferer, a lamb to the slaughter. They call us to be a bodily witness to a violent world of the powerless power of nonviolent love.

6. At least in part, the New Testament's prohibition of self-defense or self-preservation depends on the eschatological suspension of the quest for justice or retribution: that is, the conviction that things will be put right not in the present evil age but in the age that is to come, and not by human will but by God's unerring restorative judgment.

This "eschatological suspension" seems to make sense of Paul's radical view—so contrary to our present sensibilities—that "if for this life only we have hoped in Christ, we are of all people most to be pitied" (1 Cor. 15:19). Paul and the evangelists expect that life in the crucified Messiah's retinue will be cruciform, leading to suffering, even death. Nowhere do they place such value on continuing to live in "this present evil age" that they are willing to envisage armed defense. Rather, they are motivated by a robust hope in some future beyond this vale of tears, and they share with the early martyrdom literature a conviction that Christian bravery in the face of death consists in love and testimony, not violent resistance.

Whether this eschatological suspension would require one to agree with the retributive payback promised to the evildoers by God is another question, and one worth discussing in another context. But 1 Peter invokes Jesus' own hope in "the one who judges justly" as underwriting his nonretaliation in the face of suffering (2:23). Similarly, in speaking against the propriety of intra-Christian lawsuits, Paul argues against the legitimacy of seeking justice or exacting retribution at all costs: "Why not rather be wronged? Why not rather be defrauded?" (1 Cor. 6:7). One can perhaps imagine Paul extending his question: "Why not rather be killed?" More pointedly, when Paul ponders the enduring love of Christ, he forcefully denies that even violent death (by the sword!) can separate the individual from this love: "Who will separate us from the love of Christ? Will hardship, or distress, or persecution, or famine, or nakedness, or peril, or sword?" (Rom. 8:35). The hope of that enduring love underwrites the risk of nonviolence by emphasizing that death does not have the last word.

7. The New Testament does not know the Enlightenment language of "rights," but speaks of authority (in Greek: exousia) delegated by God to be used in the interest of human flourishing. Even then, in situations of the conflict of goods, the apostle Paul recommends privileging love over a private good and draws a stark distinction between the permissible and the commendable.

If the Second Amendment to the U.S. Constitution confers the right to bear arms, should the individual Christian take up that right or refuse to do so? It is instructive to consider Paul's example in 1 Corinthians 9. This chapter comes in the middle of Paul's discussion of food sacrificed to idols (1 Cor. 8:1–11:1). Paul concedes that the Corinthians who have "knowledge" are not wrong to think that "an idol is nothing in the world," and so to consider themselves in the right to eat food sacrificed to such nonentities. But Paul urges that it would be wrong to insist on such knowledge and counsels instead that the impulse to persist with eating be forsworn. He then supplies his own practice as an exemplum: as an apostle, he has the authority to insist on being paid for his work, and he is in a position to rightfully demand financial support from the Corinthians and other communities to fund his apostolic vocation. But, he says, "we have not made use of this right, but we endure anything rather than put an obstacle in the way of the gospel of Christ" (1 Cor. 9:12). The gospel and the love of others it demands are more important than individual choice. As he says in Romans 14, "If your brother or sister is being injured by what you eat, you are no longer walking in love. Do not let what you eat cause the ruin of one for whom Christ died" (14:15).

If we take this to be a statement that walking according to love entails renouncing the right of private choice for the sake of another's flourishing, we might imagine Paul addressing American Christians, in light of the tragic statistics of human devastation to which gun usage in this country has led: "For if, for the sake of owning a gun, your brother or sister is grieved, you are no longer walking according to love; do not for the sake of mere gun ownership destroy that one for whom Christ died."

8. Nowhere does the New Testament envision the state and its laws as superseding the example of Jesus or the common tradition of the church. The state cannot allow the Christian to do something Jesus forbids. Rather, the New Testament casts the assembly of believers as the determinative body of moral action, a countercultural community whose symbol is the cross.

In other words, the New Testament envisions the Christian community as the normative culture in which values and moral virtues are formed. But it is just here that we come up against one of the most troubling elements of American gun ownership. At least 25 percent of gun owners say that owning a gun is a very important part of their overall identity, with another 25 percent saying it is somewhat important.[13] This identity shaping aspect of gun ownership might call to mind the identity shaping claims of another community. In fact, American gun culture fulfills many of the same functions the church has ascribed to itself.[14] A recent sociological analysis notes that

> American gun owners vary greatly in their sense of empowerment from guns; most dramatically, white respondents who have undergone or fear economic distress tend to derive self-esteem and moral rectitude from their weapons. For this distinct group of gun owners, gun empowerment delivers a sense of meaning to life that neither economic status nor religious devotion currently provide. These owners' attachment to guns draws directly from popular narratives concerning American masculinity, freedom, heroism, power, and independence. In turn, owners who feel more emotionally and morally empowered by their guns are more likely to think that guns can solve social problems and make communities safer,

13. See "America's Complex Relationship with Guns," Pew Research Center.

14. See Richard Hofstadter, "America as a Gun Culture," *American Heritage* (October 4, 1970): 4–10, 82–85; cf. also David Yamane "The Sociology of U.S. Gun Culture," *Sociology Compass* 11 (2017): 2497 (https://doi.org/10.1111/soc4.12497); F. Carson Mencken and Paul Froese, "Gun Culture in Action," *Social Problems* 66 (2019): 3–27; Katarzyna Celinska, "Individualism and Collectivism in America: The Case of Gun Ownership and Attitudes toward Gun Control," *Sociological Perspectives* 50 (2007): 229–47.

and that citizens are sometimes justified in taking violent action against the government.[15]

Conversely, they note that "high levels of religiosity [here understood as frequent attendance at church activities] decrease gun empowerment among gun owners[,] suggesting that religious commitment offsets the need for meaning and identity through gun ownership."[16]

The gun, it seems, serves as an instrument of cultural formation; it gives to its owners by giving them each other and by helping them find a place to belong. It is interesting that we seem to acknowledge this in the way we speak: a gun transforms one into a new category of person, a "gun owner," though we don't speak with such identitarian language about, say, desk owners or knife owners. In this sense, the purchase of a gun is a sort of ritual of initiation. The gun is an invitation, a handshake, a rite of entry. And so it is, for some gun owners at least, that the cultural trappings of this subgroup of fellow gun owners have offered such a sense of belonging and community building that to raise the possibility of limitation or control of guns is to threaten their very sense of self.

We are therefore talking not merely about incidental ownership of a discrete object, but about a form of self-formation through collective belonging, mediated by the gun. In other words, the gun takes on a symbolic function that depends on but exceeds its mechanical function. It is a community centered around an object, but not merely an object in its own right—rather, an object as symbol.

What are we to make of a community whose organizing

15. Mencken and Froese, "Gun Culture in Action," 4.
16. Mencken and Froese, "Gun Culture in Action," 16.

symbol is the gun? Can it also be Christian? The Christian community, of course, already has its own organizing symbol: the cross. One is a reminder of violence suffered unjustly, while the other is a call to resist violently the threat of violence. To be precise, this would substitute a symbol of retaliation for evil for a symbol of nonretaliation for evil. It is difficult to see how they can be easily reconciled.

So can a Christian own a gun? In these reflections, I have argued that the broad shape of the New Testament's vision of bodily life in this world militates against that possibility. The Christian should be a *signum amoris*, a sign of love, marked by contrast, rather than an armed reflection of the armed world. The gun is a temptation to become a kind of powerful self, with the capacity to kill instantaneously. This is an arrogation of power that the New Testament's witness does not support, even in self-defense.

The past few years have set records for background checks for gun purchases. In 2018 the average was 2.2 million checks per month, and in 2019 there were over two million checks in each month. During the pandemic these numbers jumped even higher, to an average of 3.4 million checks per month.[17] Undoubtedly, given what we know of Protestant (and, to a lesser extent, Catholic) proclivities, hundreds of thousands of those checks were initiated by Christians. It is important to think about that for a moment. For anyone to responsibly purchase a gun (unless it is with the sole intention of, say, hunting or sport shooting), they must at some point imagine a scenario in which they

---

17. "NICS Firearm Background Checks: Month/Year," https://www.fbi.gov/file-repository/nics_firearm_checks_-_month_year.pdf.

would use the gun against a human. Maybe they imagine an intruder in their house, or a car-jacker, an active shooter, or some other kind of threat. Odds are that most people, to reach the point of buying a gun, have imagined such scenarios dozens of times. This means they have habituated themselves to these acts of lethal imagination. Many will eventually have practiced with targets outlining the human body. Their fantasized anger toward an other, the will that an other die rather than oneself, is enacted and internally reinforced again and again, whether or not they are ever presented with the opportunity to enact it externally.

How can such people meet a stranger as a neighbor? For those who look to the Gospels for guidance, will they not hear Jesus urging them to consider even dangerous strangers more dear to them than blood relations? "Who then is my neighbor?"—is that very question not something that should haunt one who carries the technology of lethal force on their person or stores it in their house? Have I imagined killing my neighbor, over and over again? Have I habituated myself to violence with the intention that I should kill effectively when my neighbor confronts me? How then can I fulfill the second commandment—to love my neighbor as myself—if I am preparing myself to kill my neighbor if I believe necessary?

AFTERWORD
C. L. Crouch and Christopher B. Hays

Where do we go from here? We know that the status quo cannot endure: The human cost of the American love affair with firearms is too clear. Tens of thousands of people die as a result of gun violence every year: that's the population of an entire mid-sized city. More than a hundred thousand more are injured: that's the equivalent of more than 650 average-sized hospitals filled to capacity with gun violence victims.

Most of these people never make the national headlines. Death by firearm has become so common, so *ordinary*, that these deaths go unremarked by everyone except the families and communities involved.

On this day in late May, the 2021 death toll is careening toward 20,000 lives. That's an average of 119 people who have died as a result of gun violence *every day this year*. There were twelve mass shootings last weekend alone.[1] These are sons and daughters, fathers and mothers, brothers and sisters.

The National Gun Violence Memorial (http://gunmemorial.org/) humanizes those who are killed by making the names, faces, and stories of its victims publicly visible. On Saturday, March 13, they included Adrian

1. Amir Vera and Hollie Silverman, "There were at least 12 mass shootings across the US this weekend," *CNN*, May 24, 2021, https://www.cnn.com/2021/05/24/us/us-mass-shootings-this-weekend/index.html.

Rios, Amanda Sampson, Amber Fullbright, Andre Green, Anthony Johnson, Kevin Nick, Ashli Haigler, Bryan Sanon, Chad Hill Jr., Charlie Howard, Clifton Paige, Cruz Perez, Daijon Dessasore, Damont Adams, DeMonte Lee, Dequan Moore, Devon Holmes, Edson Jones, Eric Graves, Eric Young, Eve Moore, Freddie Sanders III, Gerardo Ramirez, Gregory Ingram, Henry Ross, Isaiah Armstead, Ja'Aliyah Hughes, Jamaar Stevens, Jesse Valdes, Joshawn Palmore, Karen Hernandez, Kevin Clifton, Kevin Pierce, Levert Mickens, Lewis Wright III, Markus Floyd, Micah Wyatte, Michael Phillips, Mostafa Hosseini, Nicolas Hawkins, Quindovius Key, Robert Shorter Jr., Ronald Barner, Rufus Carmichael, Jae Richardson, Sean Acierno, Steven Bruer, Susana Rodriguez, Tevin Glaspy, Timmy Cruz, and Tomeeka Brown.

As Christians, we affirm that God created each of us in the divine image (Gen. 1:27). Each of these victims of gun violence was made in God's image. Each of their lives was sacred in God's sight. And as God says in Genesis 9:5, "I will seek a reckoning for human life." The disregard for human life that guns enable—the power to kill, instantaneously and indiscriminately—is incompatible with this care and concern for creation.

———————•———————

From the Civil War to the civil rights movement, the church has been on both sides of the major moral issues of American history. Hindsight illuminates both the beauty and the horror of the rhetoric that Christians have brought to these concerns: the soaring, prophetically-inspired rhetoric of Martin Luther King Jr. but also segregationists' ugly pronouncements of racial incompatibility.

As the chapters in this volume make clear, the American church is already deeply entangled in problems of gun violence. Too many Christians worship the gun instead of God, and too few Christians protest.

If the church has felt like a waning moral force in American culture, this may be because it no longer offers a compelling, life-giving moral witness. But history has shown that the church is capable of being a force for peace. As the caretaker of the biblical, ethical vocabulary that shaped Western civilization, the church has a unique duty to use it well and creatively. The church has an opportunity to be a moral force for good: to lead our communities and our countries toward a safer, more life-affirming place.

Christians raised in and involved in communities where guns are a part of daily life are a key part of this movement: you are the Christians whose friends, neighbors, and family need to hear this word.

It is crucial, with this in mind, that we be clear about what we are advocating here: This volume has no illusions that the United States will suddenly become a gun- and violence-free utopia. The use of guns in this country has a long and storied history, and many of the reasons that our predecessors owned and used guns still make sense in parts of this country. Some hunt game in order to feed their families; some kill predators to protect their livestock.

We have noted some of the ways in which the use of guns by law enforcement has been colored by our history of racism and discrimination; it would certainly be preferable if the average police officer on the street had neither the desire nor the need to carry a gun. But at some level it will probably remain necessary to delegate the use of force to the state—and so, as citizens, Christians have a role in ensuring this power of life and death is not abused. Specifically, the proliferation of cellphone cameras in every pocket has revealed how often police claims that fatal force was used in self-defense are false. Police who act as judge, jury, and executioner on the streets must be convicted and held accountable.

Authentic Christian identity is incompatible with an identity based on gun ownership. The Torah (Lev. 19:18), Jesus (Matt. 19:19, etc.), Paul (Rom. 13:9–10; Gal. 5:14), and James (2:8) all agreed that the command to "love your neighbor" is a fundamental commandment. It is at the core of what it means to follow and love God. To derive a sense of safety from the ability to kill your neighbor instantly is incompatible with the command to love your neighbor. The very capacity to do such a thing reshapes your mind and heart in disturbing ways: it is a claim to possess the power of life and death. That power belongs to God alone.

The commandment to love our neighbor also brings into focus the concept of the *common good*: the idea that we are responsible not only for the good of our family or our church but also for the good of our communities and our country more broadly. We say this out of a profound love of our country and its cities: a patriotism that hopes and prays to see this country and its people do better. Yet even those who feel exiled here must hear Jeremiah's call to God's people, that they "seek the peace (*shalom*) of the city where I have sent you into exile, and pray to the LORD on its behalf, for in its peace you will find your peace" (Jer. 29:7, our translation).

A peace based on the ever-present threat of violence is no peace at all, but a cold war and a covenant with death (Isa. 28:15). The Christian pursuit of our cities' *shalom* can thus never be *only* a matter of reducing our reliance on guns. A genuinely peaceful society, in the biblical sense of *shalom*, entails attention to the wellbeing of every member of the community—through education, safe housing, care for the mentally ill, and safety nets for those whose struggles could otherwise lead to desperation.

The call to action against America's epidemic of gun violence—and, more fundamentally, against the idolization of guns that enables this violence—is a Christian responsibility: part of our response to the command to love God, to love our neighbor, and to seek the peace and wellbeing of the cities and country in which we live.

WAYS TO GET INVOLVED

The following organizations are working in various ways to reduce and prevent gun violence in the United States. Many have local chapters, and there may be other, local organizations in your area.

50 Miles More (https://50milesmore.org)

American State Legislators for Gun Violence Prevention (https://www.aslgvp.org)

Brady Campaign to Prevent Gun Violence (https://www.bradyunited.org)

Coalition to Stop Gun Violence (https://www.csgv.org)

Everytown for Gun Safety (https://www.everytown.org)

Faiths United to Prevent Gun Violence (http://www.faiths-united.org)

Giffords (https://giffords.org)

National Gun Victims Action Council (https://www.gunvictimsaction.org)

Stop Handgun Violence (https://www.stophandgunviolence.org)

Violence Policy Center (https://vpc.org)

ABOUT THE WRITERS

C. L. Crouch is Professor of Hebrew Bible/Old Testament and Ancient Judaism at Radboud University Nijmegen and Research Associate in the Department of Old Testament and Hebrew Scriptures at the University of Pretoria. She is the author of *War and Ethics in the Ancient Near East, Israel and the Assyrians, The Making of Israel, An Introduction to the Study of Jeremiah, Israel and Judah Redefined,* and *Translating Empire* (cowritten with Jeremy M. Hutton). She is current President of the Pacific Coast Region of the Society of Biblical Literature and serves on the editorial boards of several series, including Westminster John Knox Press's Old Testament Library, for which she is writing a volume on the book of Amos.

Christopher B. Hays is D. Wilson Moore Professor of Old Testament and Ancient Near Eastern Studies at Fuller Theological Seminary and Research Associate in the Department of Old Testament and Hebrew Scriptures at the University of Pretoria. He is the author of *Hidden Riches: A Sourcebook for the Comparative Study of the Hebrew Bible and the Ancient Near East; The Origins of Isaiah 24–27: Josiah's Festival Scroll for the Fall of Assyria;* and *Death in the Iron Age II and in First Isaiah,* which won the Manfred Lautenschlaeger Award for Theological Promise in 2013.

Hays has written the Isaiah commentary in the *New Oxford Bible Commentary* and translated the book of Isaiah for the Common English Bible. Hays is ordained in the Presbyterian Church (U.S.A.).

T. M. Lemos is Associate Professor of Hebrew Bible at Huron University and a member of the graduate school faculty at the University of Western Ontario. She is the author of *Violence and Personhood in Ancient Israel and Comparative Contexts* and *Marriage Gifts and Social Change in Ancient Palestine: 1200 BCE to 200 CE*. She has published numerous articles and essays on violence, gender, Israelite religion, and other topics. She received her PhD from Yale University in Religious Studies and her BA from Brown University in Judaic Studies.

David Lincicum is the Rev. John A. O'Brien Associate Professor of Theology at the University of Notre Dame, having previously taught at the University of Oxford. He has particular interests in early Christian and Jewish biblical interpretation, Pauline literature, and the history of biblical interpretation. He is author of *Paul and the Early Jewish Encounter with Deuteronomy* and is currently working on a critical edition and commentary of the Epistle of Barnabas.

Shelly Matthews is Professor of New Testament at the Brite Divinity School; the general editor of the Early Christianity and Its Literature series for the Society of Biblical Literature; the coeditor of the Feminist Studies in Religion Book series; and the cofounder and cochair of the Society of Biblical Literature consultation on Racism, Pedagogy, and Biblical Studies. Included among her several publications are *The Acts of the Apostles: Taming the Tongues of Fire* and *Perfect Martyr: The Stoning of Stephen and the Construction of Christian Identity*.

Yolanda M. Norton is Assistant Professor of Hebrew Bible and H. Eugene Farlough Professor of Black Church Studies at San Francisco Theological Seminary. She has published chapters in *I Found God in Me: A Womanist Biblical Hermeneutics Reader*, *Global Perspectives in the Old Testament*, and Liturgical Press's new feminist commentary on *Psalms (Books 2–3)*. Norton has been featured in *Essence*, *Ebony*, and *The New York Times* for her creative worship design and innovative preaching with the Beyoncé Mass. She is ordained in the Christian Church (Disciples of Christ).

Brent A. Strawn is Professor of Old Testament at Duke Divinity School and Professor of Law at Duke University School of Law. He is the author of *The Old Testament Is Dying: A Diagnosis and Recommended Treatment* and *The Old Testament: A Concise Introduction*. He has edited or coedited over twenty volumes, including *The Oxford Encyclopedia of the Bible and Law*, which received the 2016 Dartmouth Medal from the American Library Association for most outstanding reference work. Strawn is an ordained elder in The United Methodist Church and regularly speaks and preaches at churches across the country. Strawn serves on the Old Testament Library editorial board.

SCRIPTURE INDEX

SUBJECT INDEX

abolition of slavery, 102–3. *See also* slavery
accidental (death), xvi, 1, 23
action/activism, 5, 8, 42, 48
active shooter, 11, 128
agency (individual), 89
alternatives to gun violence, x, 4, 10–11, 34
America
    and Christianity, 3–4, 6, 34n44, 58, 71, 75, 99, 120, 124,130
    and gun ownership, ix, xv–xix, 2, 5, 7, 9, 32n34, 34n43, 49, 53, 55, 69–70, 84, 86, 99, 113, 125
    and liberty, 3–4, 34n44, 54, 80
Assyria, 60, 62–64, 66–68, 79–82, 88–89
authority (power), 51, 59, 89, 96, 102n11, 104n14, 107–8, 123–24

Babylonia, 65, 69, 79, 82
ban (*herem*), 14n2, 27–28

Bible
    interpretation, 98–101, 104–11, 115–16
    misuse of, 102–4
    and violence, 6–9, 20, 22–24, 26–31, 93–94, 101, 104–5
        New Testament
            approaches, xi, 9–10, 14n4, 21n24, 25–26, 30, 59, 71, 78, 87–89, 93–96, 94n1, 94n2, 98–99, 102–3, 102n11, 103n12, 106, 108, 111, 115–16, 118–19, 122–24, 127
        Old Testament
            approaches, xi, 13–37, 14n2, 19, 19n19, 23, 25–26, 30–31, 34, 45, 52n14, 59, 66, 68–69, 78, 93–94 (*see also* Joshua)
bloodguilt, 49–51. *See also* guilt
bow (weapon), 9, 24, 63, 77–88, 91–82
burial, 52, 52n14